Further Topics in Sociology

Paul Trowler

University Tutorial Press

Published by University Tutorial Press Limited,
842 Yeovil Road, Slough, SL1 4JQ.

© Paul Trowler 1985

ISBN 0 7231 0900 1

Published 1985

Also available from UTP:

Theory and Method in Sociology: A guide for the Beginner by Philip Jones (ISBN 0 7231 0901 X)
Topics in Sociology by Paul Trowler with Michael Riley
(ISBN 0 7231 0875 7)
Race Relations in Britain by Andrew Pilkington
(ISBN 0 7231 0859 5)
Gender: An Introduction by Liz Clarke and Tony Lawson
(ISBN 0 7231 0904 4)

Preface

This book covers two areas of social science which have previously been given little attention in introductory texts: the Sociology of Knowledge and Social Policy and Administration. The aim has been to provide the reader on "A" level and other courses with as comprehensive a summary as possible within a short book of the important perspectives, theories and empirical research in these two fields. Areas of overlap between the topics have been highlighted, as have significant points of connection between them and Sociology as a whole. In particular the issues of the relationship between Sociology and science, Sociology and social problems and the debate about appropriate methodological techniques for the discipline have been addressed in some detail.

I would like to express my gratitude to Cathy Scanlan for her excellent typing work, which was completed while coping with the demands of her newly born daughter, Jennifer. Thanks also are due to Chris Baker and Suzanne Richardson at UTP for their encouragement and efforts in getting this and the earlier volume, *Topics in Sociology*, into print. If the reader can detect a viewpoint in my commentary then I accept responsibility for it, as I do for any weaknesses the book may contain.

Paul Trowler

Contents

Sociology of Knowledge

Introduction

The Sociology of Knowledge is based on the idea that our knowledge is in some measure a social product. There is considerable disagreement on the extent and nature of its social production. As to its *extent,* some writers believe that *all* knowledge is a product of the society in which it is found and that true or objective knowledge does not exist. All forms of knowledge, science, religion, philosophical thought, common sense ideas and accepted facts, are suitable for analysis by the sociologist. Other writers see only some forms of knowledge as socially produced. These are usually philosophical and economic theories and religions. Other forms of knowledge are seen as true and therefore not dependent on their social context. The Sociology of Knowledge is more limited in scope.

There are basically two views on the *nature* of the social production of knowledge. The first sees knowledge as resulting from the nature of the whole social system, regardless of the individuals who compose it. Freedom of individual thought is relatively limited according to this view. What counts is the nature of the social structure in which they are located. This view is termed *structuralism* and it includes two main variants, Marxism and functionalism. The second view on the nature of the production of knowledge sees it as created by individuals in the process of social discourse. The social structure does not exist separately from the individuals who compose it. It is nothing more than their collective ideas about it and is changed as these ideas change. Thus, individuals' ideas and meanings are very important and people are seen as having free will which enables them to actively *create* knowledge. Because of its stress on the independence of individuals' action this view is termed *action theory*. Like the other it has two variants, phenomenology and interactionism. While structuralism and action theory can agree on the definition of the Sociology of Knowledge as the study of the social production of knowledge, it is now clear that what they mean by knowledge and how they view its social production is very different.

The discipline of Sociology itself is a form of knowledge. Much of the attention of Sociologists of Knowledge has been to examine the status of sociological facts, theories and ideas as well as the methods used to acquire knowledge. Some believe that it is possible to establish true knowledge of the world through the method and approach adopted by the natural sciences. This is the view held by *naturalists*. Others question the status of scientific knowledge itself, seeing this as dependent on the social context which produced it and not true in any meaningful sense. They consider that the subject matter of Sociology is so different from that of the natural sciences that any attempt to copy their approach would be mistaken. These views are held by *anti-naturalists*. They propose that Sociology should develop different forms of knowledge from those of the natural sciences and use different methods to do so.

This chapter has two main sections. They concern theories on the social production of knowledge and views on the nature of sociological knowledge respectively. The first is divided up in the following way:

1. *Structuralism*
   i) Marxism
   ii) Functionalism

2. *Action theory*
   i) Phenomenology
   ii) Interactionism

Each of the perspectives is dealt with by outlining its theoretical basis and describing studies in which the theory is applied. The section concludes with a discussion of the possibility of a synthesis of structuralism and action theory. The second part of the chapter examines what the word science means and follows one naturalist's study and the arguments on which it is founded in detail—Emile Durkheim's *Suicide*. It then reviews the anti-naturalists' response to this type of approach in general and to *Suicide* in particular. A glossary has been provided to help with the specialised vocabulary used in this area of the discipline.

Structuralism

(i) Marxism and Knowledge: The Theory

Marx's Work
It is not the consciousness of men that determines their existence but, on the contrary, their social existence which determines their consciousness.[1]

With this famous sentence Marx states the central element of his sociology of knowledge; that men and women's ideas are not free and do not have the ultimate power to shape the society in which they live. Ideas are seen as *products* of the economic structure of society. Thus he is a *materialist,* specifically a *historical materialist.* He rejects the opposite philosophical viewpoint, the *idealist* one. Historical materialism concerns itself with:

> ... the sphere of human history, claiming that the most basic historical processes and contradictions are those of economic production and that these influence other sorts of social phenomena ... including various forms of knowledge. [2]

Idealism, on the other hand, suggests that:

> ... the 'external world' is in some way created by the human mind ... Social theories are sometimes loosely called materialist or idealist according to the emphasis they place on material relations of domination, economic exploitation etc, or on ideas, values and norms [3]

Marx argues that all relatively complex societies which have so far existed have been characterised by the presence of competing social classes. These classes are defined in terms of ownership of the means of production, the physical things with which goods are produced: land, machinery, tools or factory buildings. In capitalism the two classes are the *proletariat* and the *bourgeoisie*. The first owns little or nothing. The second owns the means of production. The interests of these classes directly conflict because the bourgeoisie seek maximum profits while the proletariat seek maximum wages. An individual's thoughts, beliefs and ideas are largely a product of his or her class position because of the different material interests the two groups have. [4] A member of the bourgeoisie will see society as a competitive struggle in which the best get to the top through their own efforts and deserve to be rewarded. A member of the proletariat will view life as unfair, the dice being loaded by fate, corruption or the old school tie. This viewpoint sees society as in need of improvement, involving a betterment of the position of those at the bottom.

The situation is further complicated because the two classes are highly unequal in terms of power in society. The bourgeoisie definitely control levels of employment, pay, housing conditions, education, content of the mass media and political power. There are not two equal and competing sets of knowledge. One is dominant and the other subordinate. The bourgeoisie is said to have *ideological hegemony*.

> The ideas of the ruling class are in every epoch the ruling ideas: ie the class which is the ruling material force of society, is at the same time its ruling intellectual force. The class which has the means of material production at its disposal, has control at the same time over the means of mental production, so that thereby, generally

speaking, the ideas of those who lack the means of mental production are subject to it.[5]

The bourgeoisie promote their class-interested knowledge as true knowledge and try to effectively quash the knowledge of the proletariat.[6] An example is the ideas of laisser-faire economists. They support a competitive free market economy, unrestricted by state intervention through taxation, health services and social security. These economists see this economic system as working for the benefit of *all* in society, bringing wealth, happiness and ease. The reality, for Marx, is that the workers' interests in such an economy are harmed. Their wages are depressed, their hours of work lengthen, unemployment occurs more frequently and they are not protected from these hazards by state provisions and safeguards such as Safety at Work Acts or Council housing.

In addition to representing the sectional interests of the bourgeoisie, these dominant ideas are a partial version of the truth. For instance, bourgeois science, even pure science, only studies those areas of reality which are of interest to the bourgeoisie and only studies them from the perspective of increasing the efficiency of production. The knowledge generated by the proletariat has the potential of being true. In capitalism it is polluted by false consciousness; untrue, distorted knowledge which results from the acceptance of bourgeois ideology. The proletariat cannot realise their full potential in terms of understanding the truth. The proletariat's knowledge only becomes pure and true during a revolutionary situation when they understand the nature of their exploitation, see their common interests and identify the potential of the future. At this point, when, in Marx's words, the proletariat becomes 'a class for itself', human history really begins. People are freed from the bonds of economic necessity and the drudgery of work. In communism, knowledge is no longer the product of the economic structure of society and one's class position in it because classes as such no longer exist. The means of production are owned by society, not any sub-groups. Thus:

> The possibility of possessing true scientific knowledge of society, systematically excluded by the structure of social relationships in capitalist society, can only be achieved by a complete transformation of society[7]

Marx sees the nature of the economy, particularly the nature of the patterns of ownership of the means of production available at the time, as giving rise to certain forms of thought. The economic characteristics of society are the substructure (or infrastructure) whereas knowledge forms part of the superstructure. The substructure influences the superstructure in important ways, particularly in terms of the dominance of bourgeois knowledge. Some crude interpreters of Marx have replaced the word 'influences' with 'determines', but Marx did not go this far. Knowledge, as well as the other elements of the superstructure (the political system, art forms, the judicial system) are influenced but not completely determined by the substructure. The superstructure has a certain amount of independence from the substructure, indeed at times it may exercise an important influence upon the economic characteristics of society. This instigates a series of up and down actions and reactions. F Engels, Marx's academic collaborator, puts it like this:

> The economic situation is the basis, but the various elements of the superstructure ... also exercise their influence upon the course of historical struggles and in many cases preponderate (ie are stronger than the economy) in determining their *form*. There is an inter-action of all these elements in which ... The economic movement finally asserts (its dominance)[8]

Indeed, if knowledge were not important revolutions would never come about. As we saw, it is necessary for the proletariat to achieve true consciousness before they find the unity and strength to overthrow capitalism. It is true that this change of consciousness is brought about by the misery of increasing unemployment and poverty which results from the relentless search for profit. None-the-less the product of these economic phenomena, the change in consciousness, is an essential catalyst for revolutionary change.

Marx's approach to the sociology of knowledge has been criticised for the following reasons.

(a) Marx concentrates on the written, well formulated knowledge expressed by intellectuals. He asumes they simply articulate the beliefs and ideas of social classes, especially the bourgeoisie.

(b) He is unspecific about the nature of the link between social structure and ideas, not really explaining *how* class interest becomes embodied in sets of beliefs. In other words the link between the substructure and superstructure is not fully explained, nor is the nature of the *inter*-action between them.

(c) Marx has a rather simplistic view of ideological hegemony, assuming that the proletariat generally accept bourgeois ideas without explaining how these ideas are spread or giving much importance to the ability of the proletariat to reject or modify them in normal circumstances. He sees people in general and the proletariat in particular as 'puppets', controlled by the strings of social structure and class.

(d) Marx concentrates on social classes as the only generators of knowledge. Other social groups may equally have their own interests and thus generate their own knowledge. Women, students, generations and ethnic minorities are examples here.

Later Marxists

Later Marxists, as well as other writers, have tried to overcome some of these deficiencies by re-interpreting the meaning of knowledge and offering an alternative view of its relationship to the socio-economic structure. Referring to (a), Antonio Gramsci, the Italian Marxist argues that not only academic knowledge, but the language, common-sense ideas and superstitions and views of the world of the common people are important subjects for study. Similarly, for Louis Althusser, the French Marxist, ideology does not just consist of the well-formed theoretical ideas but penetrates the world view of men and women, colouring their perceptions completely:

> Human societies secrete ideology as the very element and atmosphere indispensable to their historical respiration and life[9]

As we shall see later (pages 55-56) the Sapir-Whorf hypothesis argues that the language we use structures the way we think, the kind of knowledge we have. Gramsci is arguing that language, common sense and superstitions are *themselves* related to the class structure of society in the same way as intellectual knowledge. In this he comes close to the position of the phenomenologists.

With respect to (b), Marx's comments on the relationships between substructure and superstructure tend to be in the form of analogies rather than fully worked out explanations. This enables Marx to write about the relationships between knowledge and the economic base in different ways in different places. It also give rise to many different interpretations of his thoughts on this issue, including the 'vulgar Marxist' one of the *determination* of the superstructure by the substructure. Perhaps a better image is that suggested by GA Cohen:

> Consider four struts driven into the ground, each protruding the same distance above it. They are unstable, they wobble at winds of force 3. Now attach a roof to the four struts, which renders them stable at all winds under force 6. Of this roof one can say: (I) it is supported by the struts (the economic base), and (II) it (the roof, or superstructure) renders them more stable[10]

Althusser's work adopts this concept of the relationship between knowledge and social base. He interprets Marx's message as knowledge and other elements of the superstructure are independent of the economic base and only 'in the last instance' is the latter dominant. The substructure depends on the superstructure and so it is false to see one as completely dominating the other. While Gramsci discusses the necessity of the ideological hegemony of bourgeois ideas for the maintenance of capitalism, Althusser talks of the importance of the ideological state apparatuses for the day to day functioning of the economy. He distinguishes between the repressive state apparatus (RSA: the government, civil service, police, judiciary, prisons) and the ideological state apparatuses (ISA: religion, education, political parties, trade unions, the media, the family.) Through the ISAs, particularly education, the state maintains the necessary ideological cohesion. On (c), Gramsci believes that humans have more freedom of action than Marx appears to allow them. He is moving towards the idealist position of the phenomenologists in arguing this:

> Man does not enter into relations with the natural world just by being himself part of it but actively by means of work and techniques. Further: these relations are not mechanical. They are active and conscious ... Each of us changes himself, modifies himself to the extent that he changes and modifies the complex relations of which he is the heart[11]

The proletariat can reject bougeois ideology and have relative freedom to replace it with their own forms of knowledge. For this reason Gramsci stresses the dominance of bourgeois ideology, its hegemony, which may be threatened by proletarian alternatives, or by a coalition of social groups. This version of Marxism, with its greater degree of idealism, is taken up by many contemporary Maxists.

Later Marxists often reject Marx's view that each class produces its own form of knowledge (d), one of which is dominant. Some, like Althusser and Hindess and Hirst,[12] suggest that it is not individual classes which produce knowledge but the whole system of society, the mode of production. The capitalist mode of production gives rise to one form of knowledge, feudalism another. The individualistic, competitive approach to life could be said to 'fit' the capitalist form of society whereas a religious/communal world view likewise 'fits' the feudal mode of production. Marxists of the Frankfurt school (Horkheimer, Adorno and Marcuse) suggest that other groups besides the working class can develop revolutionary consciousness as well as other forms of knowledge. Herbert Marcuse sees students, subcultural, ethnic, racial and intellectual groups as bearers of a new consciousness.[13] The working class have been reduced into false consciousness by the material afflu-ence of capitalism. Only the outsiders just referred to can develop true knowledge because they are excluded from this affluence. For Gramsci too, groups of people or even individuals can develop unique forms of consciousness as a result of their situation in daily life. This is not intel-lectual consciousness but a particular world view or version of the domi-nant world view. This is sometimes referred to as a *weltanschauung;* a structured perspective on reality, including common sense ideas.

Karl Mannheim

The work of Karl Mannheim is central to the sociology of knowledge. While his approach is in the Marxist tradition it cannot be said to be actually Marxist. He is placed here, because he is closer to the Marxist position than any other. He adds to Marxism certain elements of phenomenology. His writing stresses the need to understand people whose knowledge one is studying. It also proposes that creation of knowledge within a particular social group is not just a product of that group's interests but a variety of factors and thus may take a number of possible forms. However, interests *do* play a part in the formation of knowledge and knowledge is, in the final analysis, linked to a social-structural source. Mannheim considers virtually all forms of knowledge to be socially located; relative to the social position of those who hold it rather than being objectively true. The only exceptions are natural sciences and mathematics which, at least in his early work, he does not consider to be existentially determined or influenced.[14]

The major difference between Mannheim and Marx is that the former sees social classes as not the *only* knowledge-generating groups in society. Others, not distinguished by ownership or non-ownership of the means of production, may generate their own forms of knowledge simply as a result of their common lifestyle.

These groups include generations, occupational groups and status groups and are probably best described as subcultures. The knowledge which they have is not only a product and reflection of their material interests but results from their daily activity which gives them a particular view of the world. In this sense knowledge is relatively free of economic determination. Mannheim would consider particular views and attitudes shared by the Metropolitan police to be a result of the experiences they have in policing a city like London. Their views do not necessarily reflect their own interests, merely their special life-experiences. This approach makes the study of the connections between knowledge and the social groups it comes from quite difficult. All Marx needs to do is to show how forms of knowledge operate in the interests of a particular class. For Mannheim it is necessary to use the methodology of the phenomenologists: *hermeneutics*. This is the method of putting oneself mentally in the place of the groups under scrutiny to see how it may generate a particular weltanschauung.

For Mannheim there are two broad types of knowledge: ideological thought and utopian thought. Ideological thought is that form of knowledge which broadly accepts the status quo and tends to legitimise it. This is usually found amongst those groups who are doing well out of the present system, the rich and powerful. Utopian thought is critical of the present system and proposes a new and better one. In this respect interests *do* play some part in the generation of particular types of knowledge, but there are many possible variations within the broad headings of ideology and utopia. Mannheim does not draw strict parameters around those groups which will produce ideological thought and those which produce utopian thought. He is not talking about rigidly divided classes but merely relatively advantaged or disadvantaged groups.

Critics of Mannheim have pointed out that there is a basic flaw in his work. He argues that all knowledge, except science, is the product of one group or another in society. The basic beliefs of one group may be directly contradicted by those of another and so there is no objective standard of truth with which to judge between them. This is the notion of *relativism* and is contrasted to the doctrine of *objectivism*. Marx was an objectivist. Phenomenologists are relativists because they believe that all knowledge is socially created and has no objective basis in reality. The problem with adopting a relativist stance is that one's own ideas (Mannheim's in this case) aren't any more true than other forms of knowledge, they too are the product of one's social location.

Mannheim tried to get over this problem by arguing that it is possible for free-floating intellectuals (like himself) to get at *a* truth, or bits of it, because intellectuals are concerned only with thought. Because they study the world and are not directly involved in it they have no important material interests. This fact allows them to be much more objective. Intellectual activity is more than personal judgement or propaganda, it involves the combination of several partial perspectives into one. This synthesis at least approximates to the truth, although this may not be absolute in the sense of being true for all time.

By trying to establish a middle position between saying that absolute truth exists and that no truth exists (ie between objectivism and relativism—he calls his position *relationism*.) Mannheim tries to wriggle out of the relativist trap. The problem with his form of escape is that intellectuals are not free floating with no material interest in the world. Their social background is almost exclusively middle or upper middle class male and they are therefore privileged. It seems that they are just as likely to produce ideological thought as any other group. Most commentators on Mannheim's work are agreed that his attempt to reconcile objectivism and relativism is a failure.

The theory applied

Several Marxists have tried to illustrate the relationship between elements of the superstructure, for example music, and the economic base. We will look at the work of Dave Harker on popular music. [15]

Harker tries to show that the popular song is largely determined in all its aspects by the socio-economic structure of modern capitalism: the technology of song production and the market forces existing in capitalism. As far as technology is concerned, these developments brought about an extension of the audience for popular music. They also transformed the social role of the singer, musician, songwriter and audience. For example:

> With a mike, you could accompany yourself with a guitar and subtle differences in tone and volume could still be heard. In the final analysis you could fill a football stadium with noise on your own. Once understood and applied, this last fact helped make sudden structural changes in the music industry, above all in the USA big bands came to be economic albatrosses, and were undercut by small groups and solo artists[16]

So what is generally seen as simply the product of a change of fashion or taste in popular music was in fact the result of technological developments. Similarly, the form of early recorded blues music was determined by the technology of recording itself:

> Only four blues stanzas could be squeezed onto a 10 inch 78 rpm shellac disc, and pure bands like the Original Dixieland Jazz Band quickened their customary playing tempo to fit these constraints (as players have done with the ragtime music of Scott Joplin, until very recently)[17]

The development of recording techniques made music more complex on record but severely reduced the number of live performances because groups could not reproduce the sound live. Listening to music became a privatised, alienated experience and has recently become even more so with the use of hi-fi stereo headphones. Harker illustrates how a few large capitalist enterprises took control of popular music and began to shape it deliberately. CBS, NBC, RCA-Victor and others began to censor the words so that Cole Porter's *I Get a Kick Out of You* had to have the word cocaine substituted by champagne and Hank Williams' *My Bucket's Got a Hole in it* had to have milk substituted for beer. They also changed the structure of the songs, giving them a standard form so that they could be written almost by production-line methods:

> In the average popular song, the chorus is thirty-two bars long . . . divided into four sections of eight measures each . . . In the 1950's, most pop songs were written in music publishers' offices in New York (hit factories) by a task force of writers who were generally treated like assembly line workers[18]

These white-owned song institutions were unwilling to allow black people into the industry and preferred white musicians to sing and play popular black music. Once they realised that black artists were money spinners, their prejudices were soon overcome. This demonstrates that the audience does have some freedom to express un-determined preferences, although Harker argues that this may have been greater in the early years of the industry than it is today. The power of the industry to control and standardise the form of popular song has grown with monopolisation of ownership and control in music and the media.

Harker also seeks to demonstate that the popular song embodies certain elements of capitalist ideology. His analysis of *Rudolph, the Red-Nosed Reindeer* illustrates this aspect of his argument quite well. One hundred and ten million copies of this song were sold, most of them the version by Gene Autry. Like many other top-selling songs (White Christmas, Winter Wonderland), it is on a Christmas theme. Christmas, Harker writes:

> . . . is primarily about spending money, and not working. Presents are given and received, parties are held, camaraderie (real or feigned) usually predominates in the family (which, in turn, the ritual helps sustain) . . . (but) to the millions out of work or below the poverty line, Christmas serves to underline their relative deprivation. To an important extent, then, Christmas highlights many of the contradictions of capitalist society, and it would be surprising if songs like (those mentioned above) did not articulate some of the key values (directly or indirectly) of the dominant ideology[19]

In what ways, then, does Rudolph articulate capitalist ideology? It is, says Harker, an account of human nature thinly disguised as reindeer nature. The hero was deformed (by a bright red nose) which made all the

11

other reindeer laugh and call him names. It is taken as normal that deviants should be isolated and ridiculed; the song tells us this is acceptable behaviour. It is also acceptable and normal that there should be a single authority figure to whom the reindeer community is subject—Santa. He is portrayed as a benevolent dictator. Seeing Rudolph's deformity as a potentially wasted resource, Santa finds a practical use for it; he puts it to work as a lamp in the foggy conditions of Lapland/Greenland/The North Pole. Again we see capitalist ideology in thin disguise; instrumentalism between humans (for Rudolph is a surrogate human) is completely acceptable. Finally, there is the crucial revelation:

> Immediately official approval is given, the four-faced reindeer bow, scrape and suck up to Rudolph (who, presumably, responds with a certain arrogance now). Sycophancy and implicit obedience are as socially acceptable in this kind of society as is hypocrisy— *then* how the reindeer *loved* him indeed![20]

In this case the relationship between socio-economic structure and the song is not a direct one; Harker is not arguing that Rudolph represents a capitalist conspiracy. Within capitalism, the song buying public are happy to wallow periodically in sentiment, nostalgia and fantasy. We buy the records and encourage recording companies to produce more of the same. The writer, Johnny Marks, was merely unconsciously echoing the realities of life within capitalism. In so doing, he was propagating ideology which seeks to reinforce the social relationships within that type of society.

Harker argues that the technological developments which have occurred in capitalism and the concentration of ownership of the music and media industries have combined to produce a mediated form of music which is far from truly popular in the sense of being 'of the people'. Styles are created, copied and consigned to oblivion in the interests of profit.

This analysis still leaves much to be desired. His comments about the technological determination of music are fragments of a theory, not a fully developed explanation. The record companies would certainly reply to his argument about their manipulation of music forms by saying that they are providing what people want. In some senses this is true, though what people want is often shaped by what they are given. Given that there *is* a certain autonomy in people's tastes, Harker does not explain how these tastes are developed or why they change over time and between cultures. This omission is explicable by reference to his Marxist point of view, according to which popular taste is largely a product of forces operating at a higher level. Personal preferences are only relatively autonomous and not worthy of independent detailed study. From the phenomenological perspective though, tastes and other personal aspects of everyday life *are* autonomous—in fact it is they which create the social world in which we live, not the reverse. Phenomenological approaches to the sociology of knowledge study the kinds of knowledge, ideas and tastes that at least some Marxists tend to ignore—those which ordinary people have and which seem so natural and right to them that they are not noticed. We shall examine this perspective later.

(ii) Functionalism and knowledge: the theory

Emile Durkheim

Durkheim's sociology of knowledge concerns itself with the weltanschauung which arises in a particular form of society. Durkheim argues that this emerges from the *whole* social structure not from particular groups within it. It serves to support that social structure in most cases. Durkheim, like other functionalists, stresses the society-wide, shared nature of values, beliefs and norms. This is in sharp contrast to the Marxist's description of division and conflict in society. Durkheim writes that:

> ... even ideas so abstract as those of time and space are, at each point in their history, closely associated with the corresponding social organisation[21]

This is illustrated by the fact that when blind people are given their sight by an operation they see the world not as other members of society do, as a structured and logical sequence of events, but as a chaotic mass of objects and movements. Only slowly do they *learn* to organise reality, a learning process which is conducted within a social context. Professor Tom Bower at Edinburgh University has studied the perceptions of very young babies and finds them quite different from those of adults. On the basis of laboratory experiments he has shown that babies do not share our conception of space. They do not have the notion that an object is invisible because it is behind another, that an object moved from one place to another is still the same object or that a person coming in to the room is the same person who left it earlier. They seem to believe that spatial location affects the nature of the object. To us, appearance is more important than place. Clearly, we have learned these most 'elementary' concepts during our early socialisation. The most fundamental elements of our knowledge are thus socially generated.

In *The Division of Labour in Society*[22] Durkheim outlines his theory of social change and the social generation of knowledge. In the earliest forms of society social order is maintained by what he calls *mechanical solidarity*. There is virtually no division of labour, all members of society do much the same activities. Associated with the common roles are common values and beliefs. The collective conscience is very strong. Durkheim defines this as:

> The totality of beliefs and sentiments common to average citizens of the same society (that) forms a determinate system which has its own life[23]

The collective conscience arises in the following way according to Durkheim. Whenever persons interact they develop common ideas, viewpoints and norms which become increasingly their own. These new, shared values gradually begin to exercise constraint on the individual and to spread among the wider population. Once consolidated the collective consciousness is transmitted to the new generation through socialisation and in mechanically solidaristic societies is not threatened by the need to perform any action which is not also done by most other people.

The collective conscience constrains the behaviour of individuals through taboos and imperatives. Virtually none of the individual's thoughts are his or her own personal beliefs, ideas or motivations. They stem from the collective conscience which is a *social fact,* a product of society which exercises total constraint on the individual:

> Solidarity which comes from likeness is at its maximum when the collective conscience completely envelopes our whole conscience and coincides in all points with it. But, at that moment, our individuality is nil[24]

In later forms of society a different form of social solidarity appears. This is called *organic solidarity*. There is a much greater degree of division of labour and many more social roles. The collective conscience becomes weaker because the individual's activities are unique to him or her. Ideas about correct or incorrect behaviour within the role are known in detail only by the performer. The collective conscience still exists, it has to because without it there would be no society just a collection of individuals. Now, it comprises only very general values: for example, rules about not killing other people or how to behave nicely. It does not contain knowledge of how to conduct one's daily life as was previously the case. Organic solidarity is possible:

> only if each one has a sphere of action which is peculiar to him; that

is, a personality. It is necessary, then, that the collective conscience leave open a part of the individual conscience in order that special functions may be established there, functions which it cannot regulate[25]

Social order is maintained in this form of society by the fact that each of the parts depends on the others for its existence. The remaining collective conscience is important, especially in that it includes the acceptance of the need for social differentiation.

The change from mechanical to organic solidarity comes about because of an increase in population. This leads to increased social interaction which causes competition and conflict which threatens to disrupt the social order. By pursuing *different* trades people no longer compete with each other. The division of labour reduces competitive struggle, but it also brings about a change in the nature of *knowledge*. From a socially given thing it increasingly becomes the product of the individual personality. Despite this increasing importance of the personality it is still true that for Durkheim, as for other functionalists and Marxists, individuals are the product of their society and not the society of its individuals. In mechanically solidaristic society this is obviously true; individuals are all alike, any individual characteristics they may have are lost in the totality. But even in the organically solidaristic version society is important. *It* creates organic solidarity when overpopulation threatens the mechanical form. No individual consciously or rationally decides to reorganise society in this way: it is done *to* men and women, not *by* them.

The theme of society being bigger and more powerful than individuals, the central element of the structuralist perspective, is brought out in Durkheim's study of religion. In *The Elementary Forms of The Religious Life*[26] Durkheim studies what he considers the earliest and simplest form of religion to shed light on our own. This is the totemic religion of Australian tribes. The study of religion is important not only for its own sake but because:

religion has not confined itself to enriching the human intellect, formed beforehand, with a certain number of ideas; it has contributed to forming the intellect itself. Men owe to it not only a good part of the substance of their knowledge, but also the form in which this knowledge has been elaborated[27]

Australian aboriginal tribes are broken down into clans and each of these has a totem, a symbol with which they identify and which is sacred to them. According to Durkheim these are symbols of society and the clans' feelings towards them are really expressions of their reverence for society. Periodically there are religious rituals and ceremonies which reinforce the high emotions that only social life can bring. They also integrate the society through a common enterprise and a feeling of solidarity. The collective conscience is strengthened. To sum up the argument: society moulds religion which shapes forms of knowledge. Durkheim writes:

> The general conclusion of (this book) is that religion is something eminently social. Religious representations are collective representations which express collective realities[28]

Durkheim's structuralism is brought out very clearly in this passage:

> There is no doubt that a society has everything needed to arouse in men's minds, simply by the influence it exerts over them, the sensation of the divine, for it is to its members what a god is to his faithful ... In either case, the believer feels that he is obliged to accept certain forms of behaviour ... Society also maintains in us the sensation of a perpetual dependence, because it has a nature peculiar to itself, different from our individual nature, and pursues ends which are likewise peculiar to itself; but since it can attain them only through us, it imperiously demands our co-operation ... So it is that at every moment we are obliged to submit to rules of conduct and ideas which we have neither made nor willed ... [29]

We will return to study this in greater detail in a later section.

Talcott Parsons

Parsons' sociology of knowledge is a central part of his whole social theory. Of all functionalists, his work probably contains the most all-encompassing theoretical explanation of the workings of society. He argues that for a society to operate in good order it must fulfil four functional prerequisites. This has been referred to as the *gail* model and is as follows:

Goal attainment the selection and clear definition of the priorities and aims which are to be sought by society

Adaptation to the environment, provision of the basic necessities for human existence like food and shelter

Integration of the elements of society in order to ensure proper co-ordination and co-operation

Latency minimization of the tensions which might stop individuals from working efficiently. Motivation of people to work to the best of their abilities.

The functional prerequisites are fulfilled by social institutions, each of which is merely a collection of social roles.

Parsons' Gail Model [30]

Functional prerequisite	Central sector of society	Instititutions	Examples of roles within institutions
Gaol Attainment	Political System	Political parties Pressure Groups	Leader General Secretary Party Agent Canvassers
Adaptation	Economy	Factory System Financial Institutions Shops	Manager Shop Floor Worker
Integration	Community Organisations	Church, School, Media	Teacher Pupil Vicar Editor
Latency	Kinship	Family, extended and nuclear	Father Mother Daughter

17

This whole system is underlain by a set of fundamental values, Durkheim's collective conscience. The institutions are only sets of roles. Roles are simply ideas about correct and incorrect behaviour for certain social positions put into practice. The fundamental values are transmitted through socialisation in the family and are reinforced and developed in those institutions, fulfilling the *integration* pre-requisite. When we are born we learn from our parents the central value system of our society and, later, particular values about the rights and wrongs of individual roles. Like Durkheim, Parsons sees individuals very much as puppets, controlled by society in what they think and what they do.

In some ways it might be said that this unqualified view of Parsons as a structuralist is unfair. After all, he describes himself as an *action theorist,* ie as someone who adopts an approach which:

> emphasises how actors perceive a social situation, the ends they choose to pursue in it, and the means they adopt in pursuing them[31]

His first book *was* called *The Structure of Social Action* and in it he *did* explain how actors create social reality in quite a free way. The main conclusion of that book is that structuralism and action theory can be combined, and he sees himself in his later work as doing this. Thus he would reject the structuralist label. In a very close analysis of his work Ken Menzies[32] shows that Parsons does not successfully combine these two perspectives. Parsons uses action theory or structuralism whenever either one is most useful in terms of explanation. The two are not really united. The predominant theme is the structuralist one, and this is particularly clear in Parsons' account of socialisation. The child has no independent reality; he or she simply accepts norms and values from parents and the wider society.

Menzies writes that:

> What Parsons means by a voluntaristic theory of action (is that) . . . man creates his meanings in the sense that they are not given by external reality. However, man does not create reality in a creative way (meaning a novel way). What gets institutionalized is what already exists in the cultural system. Parson's voluntaristic theory of action does not see man as free, for then one cannot account for social order[33]

The social order is founded on the common values imparted by the socialisation process. This view of individuals, as social beings whose very thoughts are outside their control, is heavily criticised by phenomenologists and others. D Wrong in *The Oversocialised Conception of Man in Modern Sociology* and R Dahrendorf in *Homo Sociologicus* conduct a heavy attack upon it.

The theory applied: Primitive Classification

In *Primitive Classification* Durkheim describes the structure of Australian aboriginal societies. In the Wakelbura tribe of Queensland the social structure looks like this:

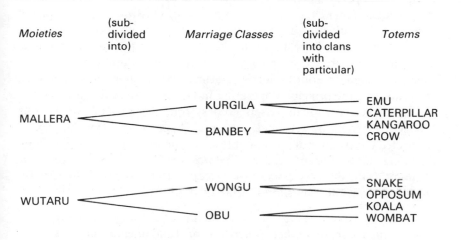

Moieties	(sub-divided into)	Marriage Classes	(sub-divided into clans with particular)	Totems

MALLERA — KURGILA — EMU / CATERPILLAR
— BANBEY — KANGAROO / CROW

WUTARU — WONGU — SNAKE / OPPOSUM
— OBU — KOALA / WOMBAT

The whole of the natural world is inextricably tied up with the organisation of the tribe. Just as the tribe is divided and subdivided, so reality is divided. The sun is Mallera, the moon is Wutaru, some types of food are in the Wongu class, others are Obu. Animals are totemic symbols for particular classes so that the clan belongs to the animal and vice versa. The people in the corresponding moieties and marriage classes will only eat food in a particular subclass of their cosmology. Similarly:

> ... a sorcerer belonging to the Mallera (moiety) ... may use in his art only things which similarly belong to Mallera [34]

Likewise:

> At a burial, the scaffold on which the (Mallera) corpse is exposed must be made of the wood of some tree belonging to the Mallera class ... If it is Banbey, a broad-leafed box tree must be used, for this tree is Banbey [35]

Other simple societies such as the Zuñi of South America and Sioux Indians have a similar system of social organisation. The classification of things reproduces the classification of people. An individual in this type of society:

19

> looks upon the universe as the Great Tribe to one of whose divisions he belongs, and all things, animate and inanimate, which belong to his class are parts of the body corporate whereof he himself is a part [36]

Because men and women were grouped, and saw themselves as grouped, they grouped other things. The two systems of classification, that of the tribe and the universe, are not separate; they are aspects of the same system. There is no logical basis to the grouping of the natural world as for example there is in biologists' groupings. Similarly, ideas of superiority and inferiority in the natural world stem only from the application of the principles operating in the social stratification system. Logic, connected thought, itself comes from the idea of connections between different objects and concepts. A particular type of tree is connected to certain groups of people and animals in that they all occupy the same subdivision of reality. The way the Australian tribesman or woman thinks, the very essence of perception, is structured by society. Durkheim concludes by stating, grandly, that:

> What we have tried to do for classification might equally be attempted for the other functions or fundamental notions of understanding ... even ideas so abstract as time and space are, at each point in their history, closely connected with corresponding social organisation. The same method could help us likewise to understand the manner in which the ideas of cause, substance and the different modes of reasoning etc. were formed [37]

The editor and translator of the English edition of Durkheim's book is highly critical of the study. Durkheim and his co-author:

> assume that which they intend to establish, viz, that a classification by groups is prior to one by reference to nature ... They claim that the astral mythology of certain Australian tribes is 'moulded' by the totemic organisation, when all that they have really shown is that stars are so part of a general classification that they may stand in definite relationships to social divisions [38]

The methodology used in the book is alien to Durkheim's preferred approach, as stated in his *The Rules of Sociological Method*. He does not use concomitant variations (see page 45) to establish a link between types of social organisation and types of symbolic classification. He frequently discusses the feelings and ideas of individuals in society, which elsewhere he argues one should not do.

More important than these criticisms is the fact that Durkheim's basic argument on the sociology of knowledge is flawed. He is saying that society determines religious thought in the earliest form of society and that religious thought is the basis of *all* forms of thinking. What is true of simple societies is also true of complex societies. The only difference is that religion has a less central role in complex than in simple societies. The problem is that there is no apparent connection between religion and the other forms of thought that exist in society. Science and religion, for example, are often said to be opposites. Philosophy, sociology, common sense, and most other forms of knowledge seem in no way religiously based. Durkheim does not recognise that there can be different, even competing, forms of knowledge within one society. This is ignored because of his insistence on the *unity* of society and hence the unity of knowledge. He cannot appreciate that particular forms of knowledge may be generated by particular social groups within society. For him society has an essential indivisibility. People in it are united by a common value system and hence produce one type of knowledge. This is clearly an inaccurate description of forms of thought in advanced industrial societies.

Action Theory

(i) **Phenomenology and knowledge: the theory**

Alfred Schutz

Phenomenology as a perspective differs from the two we have previously examined in two very important ways:

> **1.** . . . orthodox sociology has a picture of man born into a world over which he has no real control; society is something that *does* things to people. The phenomenological solution is to replace this essentially passive view of mankind with a view that stresses man's autonomy in creating his social world

Phenomenology rejects structuralism and the view of humanity as *homo sociologicus.*

> **2.** orthodox sociology is unreal and artificial and quite fails to come to grips with the real social world . . . it fails to analyse the everyday world in which people live. The fault is not because sociology (and especially the sociology of belief) studies intellectuals and intellectualized belief, rather than the man in the street, but rather that sociologists seem uninterested in the ordinary, routine

practices that all human beings engage in every day. The problem
is that the reality of everyday life is taken for granted by everybody,
since everybody, including sociologists, participates in it.

... However, this conceals the manner in which everyday life is
a constructed reality, which has to be constantly maintained[39]

So phenomenology concentrates its studies on everyday life and taken-
for-granted reality.

Schutz's work is a sociological application of the philosopher
Husserl's writing. In some ways it is close to Max Weber's thought.
Schutz agrees with Weber that sociologists must try to understand the
actor's motives for action. However Schutz stresses that subjective
meanings and motives are shared and understood by everyone in a given
society. They are not individual phenomena.

Weber discusses just one person doing an action, and the possible
motives and meanings for doing it. Schutz points out that others of the
same society would automatically share these meanings. All human
beings have a shared stock of common-sense knowledge. Now this
doesn't sound very far from the structuralist position: the common stock
of knowledge is given to (imposed on?) us by a society which exists prior
to any particular individual within it. At times Schutz sounds very like
Parsons:

with respect to the child (those around him/her) ... conduct themselves in ways which are determined by social institutions
(marriage, fatherhood, etc) and the child is apprehended by them
in socially derived typical forms (such as first born, son, blessing
of god, crutch, etc)[40]

Similarly the language we use is given to us from outside and is important
in creating a shared objective reality through the transmission of
individual subjective ones.

Although there are elements of structuralism in Schutz's thought, he
stresses people's power to create their world in two senses. Firstly, the
particular situation each individual occupies and the unique events that
happen to him or her mean that he/she must both construct and interpret
knowledge of reality to fulfil the aims which he or she has. This will be
illustrated below in our discussion of ethnomethodology. Secondly, all
knowledge is produced in human interaction, so while it is given to
children by their parents, it is also in a constant state of being interpreted
and reinterpreted. It is subject to change and re-construction by
individuals. This puts the sociology of knowledge at a central

position in the discipline as a whole. As Peter Hamilton expresses the point:

> it is in one important sense impossible to discuss sociology of knowledge as separate from sociology itself as an element of phenomenological research. For our knowledge of social and natural reality is in fact identical with that reality: as our knowledge changes so also changes the reality that it constitutes[41]

Peter Berger and Thomas Luckmann

In *The Social Construction of Reality* Berger and Luckmann present a phenomenological approach which incorporates both the view that individuals create society and society the individual.

Berger and Luckmann imagine two pre-societal persons, A and B, who interact with each other without the benefit of any social roles, expectations or other socially induced constraints. Each watches the other act and typifies the actions as recurrent after a time. Each develops views about the other and acts on the basis of the expectations they have about probable responses of the other. In this way they begin to play *roles* with regard to each other. Now their behaviour is predictable and each begins to see his role as fixed. What is happening here is the *social construction of reality*. Individuals are creating, in interaction with each other, a view of how things are.

Knowledge has been created by A and B now, but for it to survive over time, *institutionalisation* must take place. This can only occur with the appearance of a new generation (C and D) who are socialised into the roles created by A and B. C and D had no hand in the shaping of social reality and as far as they are concerned they are in a given role and have to simply accept it. So, for the generation *after* the original creators:

> institutions (sets of roles), as historical and objective facticities, confront the individual as undesirable facts. The institutions are *there, external to him, persistent in their reality, whether he likes it or not*[42]

Even for A and B the sets of roles created by them are solidified by the presence of C and D because they have to teach them how things are done.

Here we see the merging of the two philosophical positions; while society and the knowledge it contains are human products independently created, they are *also* external realities which impose themselves on individuals:

> Society is a human product. Society is an objective reality. Man is a social product[43]

However, reality (that which we recognise as having a being independent of our own volition) and knowledge (the certainty that phenomena are real and that they possess specific characteristics[44]) are not just created at the beginning of a society's life. They are subject to change as individuals subtly change the social roles which they occupy. For all of us there can be a certain degree of creativity within the context of a given reality so that:

> the relationship between knowledge and social base is a dialectical one, that is, knowledge is a social product and knowledge is a factor in social change[45]

There is only a limited scope for human freedom because there are powerful forces of social control which legitimise and sustain the status quo. Religion is important amongst these for Berger and Luckmann. One of the greatest threats to the set of ideas about what is real and normal is *death*. This, together with natural disasters, is an event which needs to be explained to individuals and incorporated into the reality of that particular society. If this is not done the order which has been created through the creation of social institutions and their accompanying reality is destroyed. Religion explains why things like death happen, describing such events as part of 'God's Will.' It also legitimises the established social order and its knowledge by portraying them too as creations of God rather than man. This process of legitimisation has in the past been done in quite a deliberate way according to Berger and Luckmann. They say that in India the ruling princes invited the Brahmins to establish the Hindu religion in newly colonised areas because they well understood its power of social control.

Berger and Luckmann reject the objectivist position, which states that reality exists independently of individuals. Social and natural reality are social constructs. For this reason any attempt to apply natural-scientific methods in sociology is doomed to failure. The position of subjects like physics and chemistry rests on the assumption that reality exists objectively out there and that we can establish truths about it which hold for all time. Neither of these propositions is true for phenomenologists.

Harold Garfinkel and Ethnomethodology

Ethnomethodology is the study of the methods used by people in their everyday lives. The term was coined by Garfinkel and is used to refer to a relatively minor school of sociology. It was developed at the University of California at Los Angeles in the 1950's and is based on the work of Schutz, with whom Garfinkel studied. Ethnomethodology is the practical application of phenomenology; its application in real situations. Garfinkel tried to expose people's common-sense knowledge to sociological enquiry. One way he did this was to ask his students to conduct experiments. They were to refuse to take for granted the common-sense knowledge one normally operates with. In other words they would refuse to share the knowledge we depend on in everyday interaction.

Garfinkel's study of jurors illustrates the way in which we depend on taken-for-granted knowledge and also shows how people actively *use* the social stock of knowledge rather than being passive recipients of it. In reaching their verdict of guilty or not guilty the members of a jury use common sense knowledge about what must have happened, what the witness meant, the motives that might have made a person commit a crime and why he/she might be telling a lie. They do not evaluate the reliability of this type of knowledge; it is taken for granted. Using it they achieve the verdict. This illustrates the autonomy that individuals have, according to phenomenologists and ethnomethodologists:

> ... in his analysis of jurors, Garfinkel demonstrates that social situations, settings and structures are not 'out there' and independent of anyone's behaviour at any given moment; they are accomplished by members in methodical ways. In talking about the 'duties of a jury', 'the problems of being a juror', 'the rules of jury procedure', and so on, members are constituting the very nature of the social phenomenon, 'a jury', is the very talk which occasions this setting. In short, members use their common-sense knowledge, their taken-for-granted methods of practical reasoning to achieve the features of the social arrangement which makes visible the organised characteristics of what they are doing[46]

The theory applied: phenomenology, education and knowledge

The publication of *Knowledge and Control* (edited by Michael Young) in 1971 saw an attempt to unite the sociology of knowledge and the sociology of education. The subtitle of the book is 'new directions for the sociology of education' and the perspective on education it proposes has led to writers making a quite justifiable distinction between the old sociology of education and this new one.

Young criticises the old sociology of education for accepting un-critically the concerns of the establishment—politicians and educators—

and of directing research effort only into paths appropriate to these concerns. Educators and politicians worried about why particular types of children fail at school and why some children become disruptive in school. They asked how the school system and the curriculum could be reorganised to stop such wastage and provide suitable forms of education for the less able child. The sociological research effort in education began to enquire into these areas. The reasons for failure were explored. Lack of space and quiet for study, large families, traffic noise, lack of resouces in schools were blamed by early researchers. Later ones stressed the culture of the working class as central among the reasons for failure. The language of these children did not fit them for educational success, their attitudes towards the educational enterprise were hostile or at best apathetic, their parents did not encourage them to succeed and did not bother to visit the school to follow their progress. This was the theory of *cultural deprivation*. The results of this research provided legitimacy to the various pressures which were building up in the world of politics and education for 'reform' of the education system and the curriculum in the 1960's and 70's. This reform involved such measures as the setting up of Educational Priority Areas. EPA's were aimed at feeding more resources into deprived areas. The policy of comprehensivisation aimed at providing greater equality of opportunity and preventing wastage of talent. The introduction of CSE and other similar courses allowed the 'less bright' pupils to work at their own pace and to benefit from an educational experience.

In doing all this, the old sociology of education had *taken* rather than *made* the issues for investigation and had accepted a number of issues. In particular it did not ask what a good education is or why we teach what we do in schools and colleges. Young suggests we need to examine the nature and sources of school knowledge as a social product, the result of conscious or unconscious choices from a variety of options, these choices having been made by people in positions of power in the context of a highly stratified society. Once the decisions are made about what counts as *good* knowledge (and therefore suitable for inclusion in curricula in schools) it is *imposed* on learners for many of whom it is alien both in content and character. From this perspective, failure becomes seen not as the inability to come up to an objectively good standard, but as deviance from a social norm:

> If logic, 'good' reasoning, asking questions, and all the various sets
> of activities prescribed for the learner, are conceived of from one
> perspective as sets of social conventions which have meanings
> common to the prescribers, then the failure to comply with the

prescriptions can be conceived not as in the everyday world of the teacher as 'wrong', 'bad spelling or grammar', or 'poorly argued and expressed', but as forms of deviance. This does not imply anything about the absolute 'rightness' or 'wrongness' of the teachers' or pupils' statements, but does suggest that the interaction involved is in part a product of the dominant defining categories which are taken for granted by the teacher[47]

Young sees knowledge as being relative. This means that absolute truths do not exist or are at least exceedingly difficult to discover. Knowledge is created by a variety of social groups, one of which is able to impose its knowledge on the others. The features of the particular form of knowledge which has acquired legitimacy in British schools are that it is literate rather than based on the spoken word, is acquired and then repeated individually rather than co-operatively in groups, is abstract rather than concrete and is unconnected with the daily life of the learner.

These elements are exemplified in an account given by Nell Keddie of a lesson on the family she observed in a classroom. The teacher tried to move away from everyday knowledge about the family to introduce unfamiliar concepts. Though the family was discussed in a group, it would be necessary eventually for the pupils to read and then write about the topic individually to gain accreditation from the teacher. The writing would take the form of a marked assignment or an examination. Statements about particular families and anecdotes about family life would score low marks, at least in the later years of secondary schools. Work which regurgitated concepts such as the extended family, conjugal roles and privatisation would score highly. In this way the knowledge which pupils have of the family is rejected as worthless. Keddie argues that the A stream pupils are more likely to accept uncritically the teacher's definition of knowledge about the family than are the lower stream pupils. When the lower stream pupil asks the question 'why are we doing this?', the teacher interprets this as deliberately disruptive behaviour. Keddie points out that teachers have stereotypes about middle class children and working class children which lead them to interpret identical behaviour in different way. This same question from an A stream pupil (who is likely to be middle class) will be interpreted as a genuine inquiry. It is a combination of these teachers' stereotypes and the common perspective shared by middle class pupils and their teachers about what constitutes good knowledge which leads to the streaming system within the school being heavily class biased.

In *Tinker, Tailor ... The Myth of Cultural Deprivation*[48] Keddie continues the attack on the themes of deprivation in working class and black culture. She shows that in imposing their definition of good knowledge on the groups, educationists adopt what she calls a vacuum ideology. This involves teachers and administrators seeing working class and black children as lacking in experiences and attitudes suitable for a good education and, in so doing, totally ignoring their different but equally good culture. One interesting cross-cultural example of this involves IQ testing. When educators give IQ tests in the West they are testing for only one form of knowledge—that which involves mathematical skills and a particular form of logic. For this reason people from non-Western ethnic groups (as well as from subcultures within Western societies) do badly in IQ tests. It is not, as the testers often believe, because they are dull but rather that they have different ways of thinking and forms of knowledge. In a paper entitled *Culture and Logical Process* in Keddie's book, Thomas Gladwin shows that one ethnic group who would do badly in Western intelligence tests have a form of intelligence which is quite different from ours. However this goes unmeasured by Western tests and would be ignored by Western educators thanks to the vacuum ideology. The Trukese, who live on a Pacific island, were studied in detail by Gladwin to discover how people learn to think and how different styles of thinking (and hence knowledge) develop. He argues that whereas we:

> seek a unifying concept which will comprehend all the relevant facts more or less simultaneously, developing an overall principle or plan from which individual steps toward a solution can be derived deductively ... the Trukese work toward a solution by improvising each step, but always with the final goal in mind[49]

This is illustrated by his study of Trukese navigators who are able to find their way from one tiny island to another when they are hundreds of miles apart and often on cloudy nights when there is no sun or stars to guide them. In these conditions:

> A good navigator can tell by observing wave patterns when the wind is shifting its direction or speed, and by how much ... (he) can even tell these things from the sound of the waves as they lap upon the side of the canoe's hull, and the feel of the boat as it travels through the water. All of these complex perceptions ... visual, auditory, kinesthetic—are combined with vast amounts of data stored in memory, and the whole is integrated into a slight increase or decrease in pressure on the steeering paddle, or a grunted instruction to slack off the sail a little[50]

As well as all this the navigator has to deal with the boat's need to change course frequently in order to catch the wind in the right way. Sailing boats cannot head in a straight line with the wind against them.

The navigator undertakes a complex intellectual task. This is quite a different way of doing things from the Western navigator's who plots a course on a chart and refers back to it during the voyage. He/she has an overall plan and an estimate of how much of it has been accomplished. He/she does not have a physical sense of where he/she is going as the Trukese navigator does. The way of thinking of the two is quite different, but the Trukese method does not count as what *we* would consider to be 'intelligent'.

It certainly does not represent the kind of intelligence measured by virtually all intelligence tests. We might refer to this kind of ability as a 'knack' ... [51]

We discount the Trukese way of thinking and the knowledge it involves in the same way as we might discount an English child's vast knowledge of football teams' successes and players over many years. Young argues that this type of knowledge is devalued not because it is really worthless but because those with the power to do so have defined it as worthless. These people include the developers of IQ tests, of curricula and syllabuses and the teachers whose job it is to transmit good knowledge.

This work is phenomenological in that it questions the status of the taken for granted knowledge which we learn at school and consider good. We are led to question these assumptions through the use of anthropological material like that of Gladwin. Cross cultural comparison gives us a certain perspective on our own ways of thought. It also considers all knowledge to be socially created by a variety of social groups (but not necessarily classes) which also have the power to *transform* that knowledge. Instead there are different types of knowledge and, therefore, different realities. We thus need to accept *all* forms of knowledge as of equal value, including those held by children in school.

The main problem with the new knowledge-based approach to the sociology of education is that it provides legitimacy and inspiration for educational practices as new teachers seize on its critique of the old ones. However, having done away with the possibility of establishing criteria for determining good or true knowledge (and having therefore acepted the doctrine of *relativism* that Mannheim tried to tackle) there is no solid foundation from which these teachers can proceed. They cannot teach Shakespeare, good pronunciation or punctuation because these are aspects of middle class culture being imposed on unwilling working class youth. Steeped in this sociology of education, new teachers fear imposing any mode of thinking upon pupils and hence resort to 'having a chat'. Syllabuses are drawn up, especially for those in the lower forms, which centre on the interests of the children themselves and allow them to select whichever areas appeal to them and to work at their own pace. Despite the good intentions, this strategy works to the disadvantage of pupils who receive this form of education because school does not exist in a vacuum but in a world which demands possession of qualifications which are awarded to those with high-status knowledge. Even where qualifications are awarded for successful completion of courses like those just discussed, they are usually seen as valueless by employers and institutions of higher education, especially when they are often awarded on the basis of continual assessment (seen as an easy option) rather than examination.[52]

For Marxist writers on education:

> Phenomenological sociology ... has little to say about structural conflict within a society, and nothing about a dialectical understanding of historical change ... It tends to ignore the material conditions of existence which, though socially produced, have become objectified and cannot be merely 'thought away' ... it encourages people to seek change through the way they *think,* instead of providing them with means by which they can change what they or others are doing ... There must be ... an actual overthrow of social relations through praxis (the revelation of knowledge through practical action)[53]

Although Young talks about a dominant social group which is able to have its knowledge accredited, he does not go into any detail on the who, how, and why of the matter. He and the other writers in this phenomenological sociology of education do not suggest the removal of that group's privileged position, but simply that we should see their knowledge as only one of many knowledges. For the Marxist there *is* an objective social order which constrains our behaviour and thought in important ways, as we have seen. To try to change this by changing our way of thinking (ie by rejecting dominant conceptions of good knowledge) is to put the cart before the horse. Marxists believe that it is social reality which changes knowledge not the reverse, as the quote from Marx at the beginning of the chapter seeks to make clear.

For some feminists, for example Dale Spender, Young has ignored the fact that the knowledge which is transmitted in schools is *male* knowledge. The authorities on most subjects are men (even in such areas as childbirth), *they* write the books, *they* explain society and it is *they* who provide a picture of the world from which women are missing, invisible:

From the position of subordination women can see that men miss much of the evidence and can construct only poorly informed explanations: women know a great deal about the world that men do not, they know a great about men that men do not know about themselves, and until women's view of the world coexists with men's views of the world, our entire system of education will be limited, distorted, sexist [54]

The female perspective and the contribution made by women in many fields is ignored. Spender mentions great but not famous scientists like Mary Somerville, Hertha Ayrton and political journalists like Mary Manley and Harriet Martineau. This is not an accident; it is in men's interests to keep these women invisible, otherwise women would no longer have the time or the desire to look after the men. There is a male conspiracy (supported by 'scientific' findings about how women grow hairs on their chests when occupying top economic positions and psychological research about maternal deprivation in children) to keep women and women's knowledge out of the important sectors of society. This has been totally missed by Young and even by Nell Keddie, a woman. 'Men's ideology', has prevented them from seeing what is to Spender an obvious point.

(ii) Interactionism and knowledge: the theory

George Herbert Mead

Interactionism began at the University of Chicago during the first quarter of this century. Here GH Mead set out his ideas about the nature of the personality and the bases of social interaction. Later writers, notably Herbert Blumer, gave his theories a more sociological orientation. Interactionism is now an established perspective within sociology.

Mead centres his theory on what he considers to be the distinction between humanity and animals; the fact that human individuals are able to reflect upon themselves, to see themselves as objects. Animals act according to their instincts without regard for the possible reaction of other animals or people. Humans too, of course, have an impulsive element in their personality but there is also a social self, the 'me', which takes into account views and attitudes that others have of us. These may be the views of the particular individual we are interacting with at the time or of the community as a whole. We cannot know how *every* individual sees us so we adopt a picture of ourselves as viewed by what Mead terms 'the generalised other'. The 'I' is our response to the attitude of others' views of our behavoiur. The self is thus a result of the dialogue between the I and the me; the latter incorporating both the attitude of other individuals and of the generalised other.

In our daily lives we take into account the views that others have of us and change our behaviour accordingly. With friends we act one way, with parents another. In the first situation one could swear and get drunk (perhaps), in the second not because this not one's 'self' as seen by parents. This is not play acting or duplicity, we simply have a variety of selves:

> There are all sorts of different selves answering to all sorts of different social reactions. It is the social process itself that is responsible for the appearance of the self; it is not there as a self apart from this type of experience[55]

Thus the me becomes a part of our personality, our thoughts and our behaviour:

> It is in the form of the generalised other that the social process influences the behaviour of the individuals involved in it and carrying it on, ie the community exercises control over the conduct of its individual members; for it is in this form that the social process or community enters as a determining factor in to the individual's thinking ... only by taking the attitude of the generalised other towards himself ... can he think at all; for only thus can thinking—or the internalized conversation of gestures which constitutes thinking—occur[56]

The individual adopts the attitudes of the social group to which he/she belongs. These groups may be classes, parties, clubs or corporations.

The discussion so far illustrates that there is an important element of structuralism in Mead's work; the collectivity determines the knowledge and behaviour of the individual. Certainly the structural component in interactionism is stronger than that in phenomenology. Interactionism stands at a mid point between an extreme structural perspective and an extreme phenomenological one because the importance of the individual *is* recognised by interactionists. Mead sees as important not only the objective social world but also the *interpretation* of that world by the individuals who inhabit it. In addition people do not just accept others' views of themselves, these views can be *negotiated*. This is best illustrated in the work of Herbert Blumer.

Herbert Blumer

(i) The interpretation of symbols

Blumer writes that symbolic interactionism rests on three assumptions:

1. Human beings act towards things on the basis of the meanings that things have for them. Things and actions are *symbols* with a deeper meaning.
2. These meanings are derived from the process of social interaction.
3. These meanings are modified through an interpretive process.

An example of the third point might be a women who accepts a lift home every night from a married male colleague. One evening he asks her if she would like to stop for a drink. They do and he starts to tell her of his marital problems. She can interpret this sequence of events in a number of ways. Perhaps he's being friendly, perhaps he's using her to articulate his problems. Perhaps he's inviting her to start an affair. The interpretation of the question 'Do you want a lift home tonight?' becomes rather difficult[57]

Blumer writes:

> The actor selects, checks, suspends, regroups and transforms the meanings in light of the situation in which he is placed and the direction of his action. Accordingly, intepretation should not be regarded as a mere automatic application of established meanings but as a formative process in which meanings are used and revised as instruments for the guidance and formation of action[58]

Thus knowledge is in a sense given, but it is also subject to active interpretation.

(ii) The negotiation of reality

Although people are acting and reacting on the basis of symbols and meanings given by the social structure, by the groups to which they belong, each person also helps to create that structure. This is illustrated by the example of a family. For the functionalist each member adopts his or her role; father, mother, son, daughter. They simply act out the role in the way ordained by society. Blumer argues this is not an accurate description. In the continual process of interaction there is negotiation and re-negotiation of one's position. The relationship between the husband and wife may change in many ways. Their attitudes to the children and their treatment of them may alter and, correspondingly, the children may themselves change.

It is clear from this that interactionists do not only see reality as given, it is also created in the daily process of social interaction. The elements of structuralism within this perspective are balanced by a view of relative individual autonomy within the context of social interaction. Interactionists differ from structural functionalists in another sense. They do not see society as a well-integrated system of mutually dependent parts. It is a loose conglomeration. Unlike Marx and the later Marxists, interactionists do not consider any one of these to be more important than the rest. One's class is only as important as one's family, perhaps even less so.

The labelling approach

Labelling theory can be described as applied interactionism. Sociologists who subscribe to labelling theory study the way individuals or groups are assigned a label and the effect this has upon them. It is believed that the attribution of some characteristics to a person or group by others usually results in a self-fulfilling prophecy. An experiment was done in an American University in which the students secretly agreed to treat one female student as if she were very attractive. Previously no-one had considered her to be so and she tended to be rather shy. After some weeks of this special treatment her behaviour had changed; she was vivacious, outgoing and friendly. In Mead's terms there had been a change in the generalised other, leading to a change in the me. More interesting than this is the fact that the other students now found that they were no longer pretending. They actually *did* consider her attractive. This demonstrates how social reality may be constructed in an interactive way, and is not simply the product of *either* the individual or given by society.

Colin Lacey's study, *Hightown Grammar,* illustrates this process in education. Acting as a participant observer, Lacey observed how the process of labelling children occurred and the results it had for their behaviour and view of reality.

Lacey notes how in the first year the pupils of this northern single sex school are all eager to work and to please the teachers. The pupils intermix freely and are not divided by ability into streams. Gradually, the process of *differentiation* occurs. This is the separation and ranking of the pupils by the teachers, done on the basis of their academic performance *and* their behaviour. Even the teacher's assessment of academic performance is coloured by the boy's behaviour. Lacey admits catching himself thinking things like 'Who's this? Oh Jones, that nuisance, 5 out of 10 for him' when marking work. After being separated into streams by this process *polarisation* begins. This is the formation of two subcultures in the school. One is the school orientated academic culture, the other is the anti-school culture. The latter are opposed to the schools norms, delighting in not doing work, cheeking the teacher, smoking and fighting. Needless to say this behaviour leads to a deterioration in their school work, thus confirming the teacher's stereotype and fulfilling his/her prophecy.

For the sociology of knowledge the important thing is the way the process of social interaction on the basis of labels (forms of knowledge) has led to a change in the nature of reality and a change in the view of the world held by the, now, anti-school subculture. From a situation of harmony and unity (in the first year) the social reality is now one of disunity, conflict and very contrasting views of the world. The boys did not simply have the label applied *to* them, but had responded to it in their own way. Thus they both received *and* created social reality.

The notion of the *self-fulfilling prophecy,* seen in operation here, is central to much of the work in the labelling tradition and it summarises how reality is created in social interaction. This is also illustrated in Jock Young's study, in which he shows how negative labels can create or exaggerate deviancy. We shall examine this work next.

The Theory Applied: social interaction; the police and drug-takers

In *The Role of the Police as Amplifiers of Deviancy*[60] Jock Young shows how society's stereotypes of the drug-taker alter and transform the social world of the drug-taker. Society in general and the police in particular view the marihuana smoker in a certain way. In society the stereotype is quite strong largely thanks to the mass media and particularly the press. It is even more exaggerated among the police who live in a relatively closed and isolated social world. The police are very active in pursuing drug-takers partly because of this exaggerated and erroneous stereotype and partly because the drug-taker:

> threatens the *reality* of the policeman. He (the drug-taker) lives without work, he pursues pleasure without deferring gratification, he enters sexual relationships without undergoing the obligations of marriage, he dresses freely in a world where uniformity in clothing is seen as a mark of respectability and reliability[61]

The features of the stereotype and the real situation, as Young found it in his study of Notting Hill drug-takers, are summarised in the following table.

Media Label	Reality
	(before deviancy amplification)
1. Drug-takers are isolated or in a loose group	1. Drug-takers exist in a close community
2. Drug-takers have no values	2. Drug-takers have an alternative system of values. They involve disdain for work, expressivity and spontaneity
3. Drugs are central to the life of the drug taker	3. Drugs are peripheral, they are merely a vehicle for the realisation of the goals above
4. There is a pusher who corrupts drug takers. Close links exist with organised crime	4. Drug supply is informally organised mainly coming from tourists and the occasional sale by drug takers themselves. There is no criminal involvement
5. Drug-takers are psychologically unstable	5. Drug-takers are psychologically stable
6. Marihuana smoking leads to hard drug taking	6. Marihuana smokers and heroin users are completely different social groups. The former has disdain for the latter
7. The number of marihuana users is small but increasing rapidly	7. The number is large. A high proportion of young people in Notting Hill have smoked marihuana at some stage
8. The effects of marihuana are extreme and dangerous	8. The effects are merely a sense of pleasure. Psychotic effects are rare and temporary

In pursuing the drug-takers the police set in motion:

a tight-knit interaction process which can most easily be understood in terms of the myriad changes on the part of both police and drug-user. Thus
  (i) the police act against the drug-user in terms of their stereotype;
  (ii) the drug-user group finds itself in a new situation, which it must interpret and adapt to in a changed manner;
  (iii) the police react in a slightly different fashion to the changed group;

(iv) the drug-users interpret and adapt to this new situation;
(v) the police react to these new changes; and so on[62]

Clearly Young rejects the structuralist notion that drug takers passively respond to social pressure. He approvingly quotes David Matza who says:

A subject actively addresses or encounters his circumstances: accordingly his distinctive capacity is to reshape, strive towards creating, and actually transcend circumstances[63]

In the case of drug takers, they evolve a set of meanings about the police's action and how the generalised other views them:

The drug-taking group creates its own circumstances to the extent that it interprets and makes meaningful the reactions of the police against it[64]

So the process of creation of social reality is important, but it must be remembered that it is done within the context of an external social structure. The actual changes which Young noted in his participant observation study of the drug takers in Notting Hill are set out on page 38 in a rather simplified form.

As well as forcing the drug-takers into a new, closed, criminal world, the police have also inadvertently helped to bring about a new social world, a new reality for the drug-taker. In this isolated situation there is no social control by normal people, thus the drug-taker's values become exaggerated:

At the same time the creation by the bohemian of social worlds centring around hedonism, expressivity and drug use makes it necessary for the non-drug-taker, the 'straight' person, to be excluded not only for reasons of security but also to maintain definitions of reality unchallenged by the outside world ... marihuana comes to be consumed not only for its euphoric effects but as a symbol of bohemianism and rebellion against an unjust system ... The marihuana user becomes increasingly secretive and suspicious of those around him. How does he know that his activities are not being observed by the police? How does he know that seeming friends are not police informers?[65]

Criticisms of this type of work are numerous. One set of critics write:

One sometimes gets the impression from reading this (interactionist) literature that people go about minding their own business and then—wham—bad society comes along and slaps

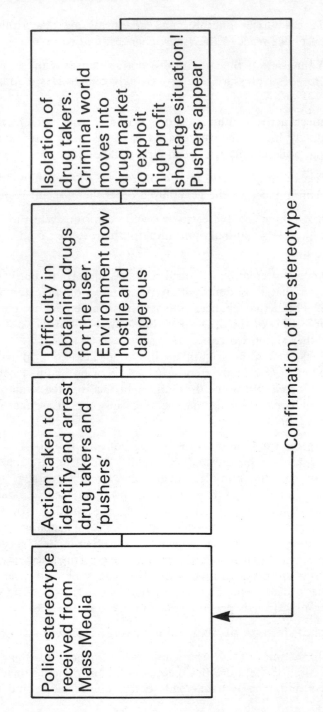

them with a stigmatised label. Forced into the role of deviant the individual has little choice but to be deviant[66]

There are two points here. One is that deviants, in this case drug-takers, must have done something in the first place to attract a label. It is not applied at random, for no reason. Given that there *are* initial differences in behaviour between individuals, some of which attract a negative label, interactionism doesn't explain why these differences exist. Why did these people become drug-takers in the first place? We are not told. The second is that interactionist writing is in fact structuralist, despite its protestations to the contrary. In many ways this seems a fair point. Certainly in Young and Lacey's work it is the surrounding social structure which seems to have the upper hand in defining the individual's reality for them.

Most criticism of interactionism comes from the Marxist perspective. Like phenomenology, interactionism ignores the wider economic, social and political forces which affect people's behaviour. It ignores the exploitation in society which creates poverty and more or less forces people to take to crime or retreat into drug-taking. It ignores the advantages to be gained for the capitalist class from organising a moral panic against drug-takers, thus encouraging people to support tough law and order measures[67]

Interactionists ignore the fact that some people are in positions of power which allow them to attach labels to drug takers while being immune from labelling themselves. There are those in the capitalist class who break laws, violate ethical and moral standards, harm individuals and the community yet are able to hide their actions or deflect criticism[68]

Interactionist work such as that of Young is distracting attention from the real issues by concentrating on the microscopic level of analysis instead of the macroscopic. In so doing they are helping the capitalist class to continue. Their work, says the Marxist, is performing an ideological function, as is that of the phenomenologists.

Attempts to Achieve a Synthesis Between the Action Approach and Structuralism

The four perspectives we have examined take a different view of the relationship between ideas and the social structure. For Marxism and functionalism the structure dominates the realm of ideas. For phenomenology and interactionism, ideas are relatively free of social structure. Social structure is nothing other than a combination of the beliefs and values of a number of individuals.

In many instances there are areas of overlap between the perspectives. They are not *completely* separate points of view. The phenomenologist Schutz has elements of structuralism in his theory, while Marx has elements of idealism in his. Some of the writers make a deliberate attempt to synthesise the perspectives. This is true of Karl Mannheim, of Talcott Parsons and of Peter Berger and Thomas Luckmann. Max Weber also tried to blend elements of structuralism with idealism in his work. In *The Protestant Ethic and the Spirit of Capitalism*[69] he shows how a new religion and its modes of thought may simply arise almost at random in any society, propagated by a charismatic prophet. These religions may have important effects on the social structure. Protestant-ism, with its stress on hard work and saving, helped bring capitalism about through the accumulation of capital, the willingness to work among the population and the belief that waste and inefficiency is wrong. The idealism here is clear, however Weber also says that the development of Protestant beliefs, after their beginnings, was influenced by the socio-economic structure. Moreover he says that if ideas are to be adopted by large numbers of people in society there must be a correspondence between those ideas and the social conditions of the day. Inappropriate religions, doctrines, ideas and values will fade away and be forgotten if this is not the case. This is an example of the structuralist element to be found in Weber's work. Social phenomena are produced, according to Weber, by an *interaction* of knowledge and socio-economic structure. Neither determines the nature of the other, both are relatively free to move in any direction.

How successful are the attempts to synthesise competing perspectives? Peter Hamilton, in discussing Berger and Luckmann's effort, is quite dismissive.[70] He believes that functionalism and Marxism are irreconcil-able. Berger and Luckmann in fact go for the functionalist view without admitting it. Religions are not ideologies as far as they are concerned, because ideologies, in Marx's sense, operate in the interests of some and against the interests of others. In Berger and Luckmann's scheme of things the role of religion is to sustain the universe of meaning (the socially constructed reality) of any given society. Just as the universe of meaning is shared by all, so all share the religion. Berger and Luckmann have no conception of conflicting groups in society.

If there are fundamental tensions between functionalism and Marxism, what of the microscopic, actor-based, approach of phenomenology on the one hand and structuralism on the other? We saw that the attempt to reconcile *these* two viewpoints got Mannheim into difficulties. Phenomenologists are happy to concede that no truth or reality exists other than that which is created in a given social context.

As a corollary phenomenologists can do no more than describe the reality of a particular society, they cannot explain it in any sense. For structuralists, like Marx, there *is* an objective reality which can be studied and explained. Mannheim is left in the position of trying to reconcile the two views: the impossibility of establishing one truth and the potentially fruitful scientific quest for it. His compromise, relationism, has been the object of heavy criticism.

As for Parsons' attempt to unite action theory with structural-functionalism, we saw that he too falls on one side of the fence rather than achieving a synthesis. He is a structuralist. Action theory sees the individual as a free agent, able to construct reality and behave at will. Methodologically this implies that to understand behaviour we must understand the motives for action by the use of verstehen (or *hermeneutics* as it is sometimes called), empathising with the attitude of an individual. Structuralism sees the individual as constrained by society. He or she is a puppet, homo sociologicus. The method structuralism favours is the scientific study of the whole social structure, ignoring the motives of individuals within it. Parsons tries but fails to see people both as free and as chained. He comes to see them as chained.

Weber made a better attempt at resolving this dilemma. Just as ideas can change the social structure, so social structure has an effect on ideas. This interaction of opposing elements which results in change, a dialectic, sees neither as dominant, as Marx and later Marxists' work does. Weber's work is an explicit answer to Marx in this respect.

Weber seems to reconcile action theory and structuralism successfully. How does he reconcile the opposing methodological implications, hermeneutics on the one side and positivism on the other? He says that we, as sociologists, should use both approaches. We must try to understand the meanings behind social action. At the same time we must explain the working of social structure in an objective way, a way verifiable by others. To do this one constructs ideal types, descriptions of reality which exaggerate some aspects of it and omit others. This involves *selection* of the important and the unimportant on the part of the researcher, but this is unavoidable. For example, Weber's description of the Protestant Ethic and the Spirit of Capitalism are ideal types which bring out their essential features (as Weber sees them). The researcher is then in a position, having simplified certain aspects of reality, to conduct an enquiry into the effects that one has on the other. By using hermeneutics the causal connection between the two factors can be identified. Weber explained the absence of the spirit of capitalism in India by reference to the lack of any equivalent of the Protestant Ethic there. If this procedure is not possible the researcher can *hypothetically* alter one of the elements to put his/her hypothesis to the test. In other words one imagines 'would this have happened if ...?' The imagining of events can be compared with the real sequence to assess whether the hypothetically changed factor did make any difference. What would have happened *if* Martin Luther and John Calvin had never been born and the Protestant Reformation never happened? Would capitalism have come about in a Catholic environment? Clearly this presents a number of problems. The fact that we can really only make an informed guess at what would have happened is one principle objection. The fact is that Weber recognises these objections and answers them in what Raymond Aron, at least, considers to be a convincing way.[71]

Weber sidesteps the trap of relativism that Mannheim fell into in the following way. He argues that a reality does exist, he is an objectivist. At the same time he says that because we are all located in a social position we cannot see it. Even intellectuals cannot do so. What we *can* do is to uncover slices of reality by the method just described. We can never see all of it but we can achieve a slightly clearer view.

Weber unites the ideas of the person as chained and as free and deals with the apparently contrasting methodological implication each has for sociology. The next section will examine the question of science, social science and social scientific methods in more detail.

Sociology and the Natural Sciences

Definition and an idealised account of the scientific approach

The word science has been defined as:

> the systematic, objective study of empirical phenomena and the resultant bodies of knowledge[72]

The natural sciences comprise the disciplines of physics, chemistry, biology and related disciplines such as astronomy, geology, zoology and medicine. The common features of the scientific approach are set out below.

1. The search for natural laws, statements which express a relationship between two general conditions or events. This relationship must hold true for all time and in every place.
2. A consistent, systematic approach to the search for laws. Ideally the process resembles the diagram on the facing page. Objectivity is important in this process. At the stage of *observation* bias could lead to selective selection and perception of phenomena. At the stage

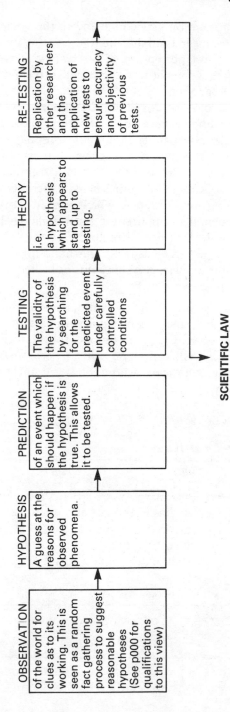

OBSERVATION of the world for clues as to its working. This is seen as a random fact gathering process to suggest reasonable hypotheses (See p000 for qualifications to this view)

HYPOTHESIS A guess at the reasons for observed phenomena.

PREDICTION of an event which should happen if the hypothesis is true. This allows it to be tested.

TESTING The validity of the hypothesis by searching for the predicted event under carefully controlled conditions

THEORY i.e. a hypothesis which appears to stand up to testing.

RE-TESTING Replication by other researchers and the application of new tests to ensure accuracy and objectivity of previous tests.

SCIENTIFIC LAW

of hypothesis formation bias could lead to the scientist missing the truth. During testing bias might lead to the setting up of a favourable test or might distort perception of the results. Bias in favour of a particular hypothesis might lead the scientist to cling to it in spite of unfavourable test results.

The methodology employed in the process of testing is very important. Conditions must be strictly controlled. *Quantification,* the ability to express quantity in numerical terms, is clearly vital to this process and this has come to be seen as one of the most important features of the scientific method. Another is the use of a *control,* ie a duplicate of the thing being experimented on in every way except one. Any differences which appear between the control and the experimental group after the experiment has been conducted *must* be a result of that one difference.

3. This process of research leads to the building up of a body of publicly available knowledge. This helps us to better understand the world in which we live.

This is an idealised account of the scientific method which has been the subject of criticism and amendment from various sources. Nonetheless many social scientists have used it as a model for the social as well as the natural sciences. We shall call these writers *naturalists.* One famous naturalist was Emile Durkheim, whose study of suicide is a classic in naturalistic sociology.

Naturalistic sociology: Durkheim on suicide

Suicides in England and Wales [73]

1979	1980	1981	1982
4,195	4,321	4,419	4,279

The majority of suicide victims in this country are male, but the rate for females is rising each year. Between 1960 and 1976 there was a decline in the overall rate, but since 1976 there was a slow increase until 1982. The following is an international comparison of suicide figures:

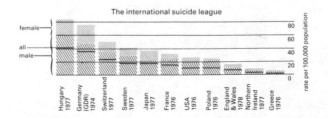

Durkheim sets out his theory of suicide in the book *Le Suicide* (1897) and simultaneously demonstrates his commitment to the scientific approach. First he examines the hypotheses that suicide may be explained by reference to the physical or psychological make-up of individuals or by the nature of their physical environment. His method of testing these hypotheses is always the same. The method is concomitant variations, closely related to a more recent statistical technique called factor analysis or, more irreverently, 'number crunching'. Concomitant variations refers to the identification of a correlation between two factors, A and B. In this case A is the suicide rate and B relates to the hypothesised 'cause' of suicide. Examples of each are taken from a number of countries or areas or for different years.

Using concomitant variations to test whether insanity is the cause of suicide [74]

	Factor A No. of suicides per 1,000,000 inhabitants	Factor B No. of Insane per 1,000,000 inhabitants	Ranking order of countries for Insanity	Suicides
Norway	107	180	1	4
Scotland	34	164	2	8
Denmark	258	125	3	1
Hanover	13	103	4	9
France	100	99	5	5
Belgium	50	92	6	7
Wurtemberg	108	92	7	3
Saxony	245	67	8	2
Bavaria	73	57	9	6

adapted from P.74 *Suicide* E Durkheim RKP 1979, first published in England 1952. Figures for suicide and insanity came from a variety of years, ranging from 1846 to 1861.

He concludes that:

On the whole it appears that there are many suicides where the insane and idiots are numerous, and that the inverse is true. But there is no consistent agreement between the two scales which would show a definite causal relationship between the two sets of phenomena

Similarly he dispenses with a number of other factors which had been proposed as causes of suicide: alcoholism, racial type, height, age, climate, imitation. He completes the first section of the book by saying:

We have ... shown that for each social group there is a specific tendency to suicide explained neither by the organic-psychic constitution of individuals nor the nature of the physical environment. Consequently, by elimination, it must depend on social causes and be in itself a collective phenomenon ... (p145)

However, he *can* demonstrate positive correlations between the number of Protestants in a region and the suicide rate there by comparing different regions. Conversely the more Catholics there are, the lower the suicide rate. Jews have the lowest suicide rate of all three religions.

	Average of suicides per 1,000,000 inhabitants 1840-1870
Protestant states	190
Mixed states	96
Catholic states	58
Greek Catholic states	40 [75]

Similarly there are positive correlations between a high suicide rate and being unmarried and living in urban areas. The common factor linking Protestants, unmarried people and those in cities is their lack of social integration. Protestantism is a faith which leaves the individual alone in front of God, there is little in the way of support or mediation by the church through rituals, confession and mass. The bonds between individual Protestants are said to be weaker than those between Catholics. Similarly unmarried people and city dwellers have comparatively few social bonds. Thus Durkheim concludes that:

> Suicide varies inversely with the degree of integration of the social groups of which the individual forms a part

We could call this Durkheim's law of suicide: *if* social bonds are weak *then* the individual is more likely to commit suicide.

This law helps explain not only the correlations we have just discussed, but also:

1. the fact that suicide rates don't fluctuate sharply (because social integration is relatively constant)
2. why different societies have such widely different rates (East Germany's rate is 12 times that of Greece at the moment)
3. why different groups within one society have different rates.

Durkheim's theory is a little more complex than this in that he identified three types of suicide. The first is caused by lack of social isolation and he called this *egoistic* suicide. It is the one we have just examined. Social integration is necessary because:

1. When society is strongly integrated, it holds individuals under its control, considers them at its service and thus forbids them to dispose wilfully of themselves

2. man cannot live without attachment to some object which transcends and survives him ... The individual alone is not a sufficient end for his activity. He is too little ... When, therefore, we have no other object than ourselves we cannot avoid the thought that our efforts will finally end in nothingness[76]

The second is the exact opposite, it is caused by *too much* social integration and is not subject to Durkheim's law. This is *altruistic* suicide. Altruism means regard for others as a principle for action. Altruistic suicide is committed out of regard for one's social group. Examples of this are the old Indian practice of *sati* in which a widow throws herself on to her dead husband's funeral pyre, or the Japanese *kamikaze* pilot who sacrifices his own life for the emperor and the nation. Durkheim seeks to prove his explanation of this form of suicide by demonstrating a correlation between high suicide rates and membership of the highly integrated military battalions. By a process of deduction he concludes that the suicides result from the group being *too* highly socially integrated:

the soldier kills himself at the least disappointment, for the most futile reasons, for a refusal of leave, a reprimand, an unjust punishment, a delay in promotion, a question of honour, a flush of momentary jealousy or even simply because other suicides have occurred before his eyes or to his knowledge[77]

The third type of suicide *does* conform to Durkheim's law and is very similar to the first (indeed, some have said indistinguishable from it.) This is *anomic* suicide. Here a sudden change in an individual's social position (through economic crisis or sudden wealth) leads to normlessness and then suicide. Again Durkheim uses concomitant variations, this time comparing the suicide rate in periods of boom, slump and in normal periods in different areas. The suicide rate is higher in slump *or* boom than normal periods, so it is not economic loss which leads to the suicide. In normal individuals desires and passions are regulated by society through socialisation. We internalise an upper and lower limit to the possessions or lifestyle we can expect from life. These limits may rise or fall slowly over time, but if we are thrown into a position where we can or must live above the top or below the bottom line we become maladjusted and suffer. In a time of slump the people who do worst:

are not adjusted to the condition forced on them, and its very prospect is intolerable; hence the suffering which detaches them from a reduced existence even before they have made trial of it

In time of boom:

Appetites, not being controlled by a public opinion become disoriented, no longer recognise the limits proper to them[78]

The individual is lost and has no firm guidance from the community. As a result there is a much stronger chance than normal of such an individual committing suicide.

Durkheim's view of anomic suicide seems supported by the suicide statistics of 1932, when the suicide rate did indeed sharply increase. Similarly the idea of egoistic suicide seems confirmed by the fall in the rate of suicide during World Wars I and II, presumably periods of high social integration.

Durkheim, then, tried to emulate the natural sciences in his study of suicide. He:

1. Identified 'Durkheim's law' by
2. a process involving; observation (of suicide statistics of various countries and social groups), hypothesis formation, establishing a prediction resulting from the hypothesis, and finally testing it and re-testing it in different areas over different times and in different ways. The idea that social integration is the cause of suicide is tested by looking at the suicide rates of a whole variety of groups with high and low integration. His methodology in doing this was a rigorous *comparative method* using quantitative data.
3. he considered the work a contribution to a general functionalist analysis of society and hence as part of a general effort to establish a body of knowledge.

Let us now examine some of the arguments raised by those sociologists who believe that their discipline should *not* emulate the natural sciences; the *anti-naturalists*.

The anti-naturalists' response to the idea of a social 'science'

Anti-naturalists, often subscribing to action theory, argue that sociology should not seek to emulate natural science in approach, methodology or ultimate aims. They insist that social reality and physical reality are quite different and that while causal explanation may be possible in the latter it is not in the former. Human beings have free will and we cannot talk of their behaviour as caused by anything other than this will. Beyond this very general point there are a number of issues and it is probably easiest to deal with each in turn. They are:

1. Sociologists cannot rely on the raw data available to them. It is of a different type to that available to natural science.
2. Sociologists have to use different methodological tools to the natural scientist. Quantification, at least in a fixed and precise sense, is impossible.
3. Objectivity in sociology is impossible. Sociologists are socialised into a partiality from which they cannot escape.
4. To explain behaviour in the physical world a natural scientist need only establish regularities and give reasons for them. Social scientists must refer to meanings, emotions and desires. They are unobservable and unquantifiable. The strongest form of this argument holds that no social reality exists *other* than in terms of the meanings held of it by social actors.
5. Sociologists cannot hope to establish scientific laws because human beings do not act in a regular, predictable way and because the reality they inhabit is created, not given, and is transitory.

In this section we will deal with each of these arguments, relating them to Durkheim's study of suicide to clarify them.

1. *Sociologists cannot rely on the raw data available to them as natural scientists can*

Robert Merton in *Social Theory and Social Structure* makes the point that:

> Despite the etymology of the term (ie its origins, the word comes from the Latin 'to give'), data are not 'given' but are 'contrived' with the inevitable help of concepts [79]

Much of the criticism of Durkheim's work has centred on his uncritical acceptance of the suicide statistics he used to establish correlations between levels of social integration and suicide rates. Durkheim accepted these data as factual and accurate records of the number of suicides committed. However Maxwell Atkinson [80] shows that coroners, who determine the cause of a death, have a common sense theory of suicide which influences their findings. Their interpretation of the death will be influenced by a number of factors. A suicide note is one factor. The mode of death is a second important clue for the coroner, the biography of the deceased (history of mental illness, divorce, deaths in the family) a third. Recent events in the individual's life, threats to commit suicide and the comments of friends and relatives are also important. The suicide statistics are not an objective record of the number of suicides but result from the interpretations placed upon a death by the coroner. Some deaths will be seen as suicide which were not, some which do not fit the coroner's model of typical suicide will be recorded as accidental death or in some other way. The suicide statistics of different countries are even more problematic. In some countries cultural differences may mean that a suicide verdict has very little stigma (Japan) or a lot (Italy) and this may result in a differential likelihood of recording a suicide verdict in these countries. In Sweden and Denmark suicide is *presumed* unless there is evidence to the contrary, which helps to explain their high rates.

There is another sense in which data are not really given. That is in the choice of data made by the sociologist, indeed in the choice of subject for study.

Werner Stark, a sociologist of knowledge, writes:

How is it ... that the research worker turns to some one definite problem among the thousands possible to him in his science? It must somehow have stimulated his interest to a higher degree than other questions[81]

Having chosen the subject of study the researcher then selects from the data available. Like the selection of the *problem,* this selection too depends upon the interests and concerns of the researcher. Durkheim's choice of suicide as a topic for study must have been motivated by his concerns about it. The sociologist does not simply observe reality and then arrive at a hypothesis. That observation is guided by interests and concerns. The data collected, as a result, has been pre-processed by these concerns.

2. *Sociologists have to use different methodological tools to those available to natural scientists. Results are not quantitative*

The table (on pages 52 and 53) summarises the main methods available to sociologists. Naturalists generally speaking prefer those on the left of the table. The more qualitative methods allow too much room for the subjective interpretation of data, they generally relate to such small numbers of people that their results cannot be said to be representative of the whole population. The use of unstructured interviews and open-ended questionnaires mean that results are difficult to collate as the researcher is left with a number of individual and unique replies which cannot be categorised into a set of results.

The anti-naturalists reply that even those methods on the left of the table are inadequate for a proper scientific approach. Controlled experiments are nearest to scientific methodology, but in the study of society they raise special problems. One is the question of ethics. Rosenthal and Jacobson in *Pygmalion in the Classroom*[82] studied the effect of teachers' beliefs that certain named students in a class were soon to undergo a leap in academic performance. Comparing the performance of the named pupils with that of a control group of ordinary pupils over a two year period, Rosenthal and Jacobson found that the performance of the former did improve more quickly than the latter. There had been a self-fulfilling prophecy in operation. A further crucial test would have been to tell the teachers that other pupils would perform *badly* but the researchers felt they could not jeopardise the school career of some pupils by conducting this test. A second problem with the experimental method is the number and complexity of the variables in a social, compared to a physical environment. There are so many possible differences between a control and an experimental group in a social situation that it is virtually impossible to say which one caused the differences between the two groups. Psychological differences between individuals or groups of them cause particular difficulties. The editor of Durkheim's *Suicide* writes that Durkheim did not attempt to isolate *emotional* differences between individuals which would account for different suicide rates:

> Reliable statistics on suicide cannot be compiled unless we have ready-at-hand accurate and painstakingly recorded psychiatric life histories on all[83]

Similarly the other methods available to social scientists have considerable drawbacks. Interviews and questionnaires have problems concerning the size and representativeness of the sample. The interviewer's appearance or accent may affect the respondents' answers. Questions may be interpreted differently by respondents, or even misunderstood by some. Those people who agree to answer the questions may be unrepresentative of the population at large; particularly a problem when the response-rate is low. Questions may be answered jokingly or untruthfully. Non-participant observation suffers from the Hawthorne effect (the effect of the presence of the observer on the behaviour of the observed) and, even with time sampling, the impracticability of observing large numbers of people usually result in unrepresentative data based only on small groups. The use of official statistics is fraught with all kinds of problems, as our discussion of Durkheim's use of suicide statistics has shown. Crime statistics are, if anything, even more unreliable. There are varying reporting rates for

Methods of Data Collection Available to the Sociologist

More Quantitative (preferred by naturalists)	Type	More Qualitative (preferred by anti-naturalists)
Controlled Experiments emulate the natural sciences by attempting to keep all factors constant in a control and in the experimental group, changing only one factor in the latter to assess its effect. eg Rosenthal and Jacobson *Pygmalion in the Classroom* *The Comparative Method* involves the comparison of two societies or groups to isolate the causes of differences between them. Factor analysis can be used (see page 45) eg E Durkheim *Suicide*	EXPERIMENT	*Uncontrolled Experiments* put the hypothesis to the test but do not attempt to control variables or quantify results. eg the experiment by Garfinkel's students to assess the effect of *not* taking for granted common sense knowledge (see page 25)
Sample Survey[84]		Small Group
Structured Interviews involve answering pre-set questions. They are really an administered questionnaire. Consistency of questions allows easy collation. eg J Goldthorpe and D Lockwood *The Affluent Worker* *Closed Ended Questionnaires* have yes-no or 'spectrum' alternative answers (eg strongly agree, agree, don't know, disagree, strongly disagree) eg P Willmott *Adolescent Boys of East London*	ASKING QUESTIONS interviews require the presence of a researcher. Questionnaires can be completed without one present. Usually they are handed out or sent by post to the home or workplace.	*Unstructured Interviews* are like a directed conversation. Points are followed up and interesting avenues explored. They may take the form of LIFE HISTORIES in which the interviewee tells his/her autobiography. eg H Gavron *The Captive Wife* *Open Ended Questionnaires* allow the respondent to write at length in answer to a question. eg D Wedderburn and R Crompton *Workers' Attitudes and Technology*

Non Participant Observation involves taking detailed notes observed as a detached researcher viewing events. More objective and reliable is the TIME SAMPLE METHOD, one version of which involves a grid along one axis of which are the events which could occur and along the other is a time scale. The observer simply indicates on the grid (by crosses or ticks) which events occurred and their duration.

Official Statistics are useful to naturalists and include those collected by the Central Statistical Office from the police, doctors, the census, household surveys and so on. eg E Durkheim's *Suicide*

OBSERVATION

Participant Observation involves becoming one of the actors being studied, involving oneself in their everyday life for weeks, months or even years. Notes recording one's experiences are made, usually daily. These are impressionistic. *Ethnography* refers to the detailed description of a culture or subculture, usually using this method. eg H Beynon *Working for Ford*

OFFICIAL RECORDS AND OTHER SECONDARY DATA (ie data not collected first hand by the researcher)

Diaries, letters, personal accounts of events, newspapers etc. are assessed by the sociologist for any insights they may contain. eg P Willmott *Adolescent Boys of East London* (Diaries) different types of crime, different levels of police activity in particular areas and against particular types of crime, differing chances of the police merely cautioning rather than prosecuting in certain circumstances. In short crime statistics like other statistical sources are highly unreliable. They reflect social processes, not the facts.

3. *Sociologists can't be objective when they study society*

There are three main levels on which sociologists can be said to be subject to bias. Firstly in terms of personal prejudices, political viewpoints, preferences and sympathies. Secondly in terms of the *perspective* adopted by the sociologist. Thirdly in terms of the weltanschauung which individual socialisation has imbued. This may be the world view of, say, a European as against an American Indian or of a member of the middle class as against the working class.

Personal biases of the sociologist are often said to be evident in the writing of socialist and Marxist sociologists. Their political standpoint is said to influence selection and perception of subjects of study and their conclusions. For example, Huw Beynon's account of *Working for Ford* is permeated with a sense of outrage at the conditions the men at Halewood worked under and of Beynon's sympathy for them. Conversely Elton Mayo's study of the Hawthorne factory in Chicago was conducted with WJ Dickson, Head of the Employee Relations Research Dept of the Western Electricity Co (which owned the plant.) Their aim was to increase productivity and their aims and conclusions, which led to the human relations school of management, are seen by Marxists and others as pro-management. Another example is Ann Oakley's explicit partiality:

> A vast number of books have been written about men and their work; by contrast, the work of women has received very little serious sociological or historical attention. Their unpaid work in the home has scarcely been studied at all. This book is an attempt partially to redress this balance. Its perspective is feminist; it challenges the set of conventional values which label work a masculine activity and assign women to the home[85]

The natural scientist does not have views about the subject of study in the same sense and is disinterested in the outcome of the study. This objectivity as we saw earlier is said to be vital for any scientific work.

The perspective adopted by a sociologist is crucial in determining the nature and outcome of the work. Each perspective involves certain assumptions about the nature of social reality and these are untested.

Such a foundation to research makes any work based on these assumptions unscientific. We have already noted (Page 39) that in the study of deviance interactionists tend to *assume* that individuals who become labelled as deviant are, initially, little different from anyone else. Another bias involved in the interactionist perspective is the emphasis on the microscopic level of interpersonal action. This may result in wider social, economic and political forces which affect people's behaviour being overlooked. Conversely structuralists may be blind to the importance of motivated action in society.

The weltanschauung of the researcher is the third level of bias. Alvin Gouldner refers to sociologists' *domain assumptions:*

> Domain assumptions about man and society might include, for example, dispositions to believe that men are rational or irrational; that society is precarious or fundamentally stable; that social problems will correct themselves without planned intervention ... They are an aspect of the larger culture that is most intimately related to the postulations of theory ... they are often resistant to 'evidence' ... to understand the character of Academic Sociology we have to understand the background assumptions with which it operates [86]

Even the language we learn as young children may structure the way we perceive the world and make us blind to some evidence, or make us feel that some theories are intuitively convincing. This is the argument put forward by two linguists, Edward Sapir and Benjamin Lee Whorf, who proposed the *Sapir-Whorf Hypothesis.* This says that the language we use sets up a kind of grid through which we perceive the world. It forces our gaze on the world in certain directions, focussing clearly on some elements, seeing others in only a blurred way. It is very difficult, though probably not impossible, to see the world other than in the way guided by the language. Peter Trudgill in *Sociolinguistics* gives this example to illustrate:

> European languages ... make use of tenses. Their usage is by no means identical, but it is usually not too difficult to translate, say, an English form into its equivalent in French or German. Some American Indian languages, on the other hand, do not have tenses, at least as we know them. They may, however, distinguish in their verb forms between different kinds of activity which European speakers would have to indicate in a much more roundabout way. Verb forms, for instance, may be differentiated according to whether the speaker is reporting a situation or expecting it, and

according to an event's duration, intensity or other characteristics. It would not be too surprising, therefore, if the world-view of a people whose language does not 'have tenses' were rather different from our own: their concept of time, and perhaps even of cause and effect, might be somewhat different[87]

Dale Spender in *Man Made Language* shows how English imposes a male-centred view of the world. For example we use the word 'man' and 'mankind' as a general term for humanity, 'he' for an unspecified person. This gives us an image of a *male* doing all the important things, and having all the important things happen to *him*. Spender approvingly quotes another author

> In practice, the sexist assumption that man is a species of males becomes the fact. Erich Fromm certainly seemed to think so when he wrote that man's 'vital interests' were 'life, food, access to females, etc.' Loren Eisley implied it when he wrote of man that 'his back aches, he ruptures easily, his women have difficulties in childbirth ...' If these writers had been using *man* in the sense of the human species rather than males, they could have written that man's vital interests are life, food and access to the opposite sex and that man suffers backaches, ruptures easily and has difficulties in giving birth[88]

Similarly the phrase 'man, being a mammal, breast feeds his young', appears humorous. Spender points out some of the *absences* in the English language which result from the sexism which it both incorporates and propagates. Males are virile and potent, but there is no female equivalent (except derogatory ones like nymphomaniac). We think of the sex act as 'penetration', but from a female perspective it would be seen as 'enclosure'. This constraining influence of the language, and domain assumptions in general mean that observation is *preceded* by theory, that we cannot observe the world in a neutral way.

Durkheim's study shows clear evidence of personal bias, perspective bias and domain assumption bias. On the personal level, Durkheim regrets the loss of the community of pre-individual society and has, generally, a very conservative outlook. Referring to the loss of community which came with geographical and social mobility he asks 'Is this *evil* then incurable?'

His perspective, a positivist and functionalist one, leads him to ignore individual motives and reasons for suicide and to stress the disruptive effects (as he sees them) of too little or too much social integration. His domain assumptions are those of a Nineteenth Century Frenchman. His attitude to suicide is quite different to that of, say, a Japanese. His notion of the 'correct' level of social integration is very different to that of a member of a religious silent order. His views on women are very different to those of a modern-day feminist, as this quotation shows:

> Man is much more highly socialised than woman. His tastes, aspirations and humour have in large part a collective origin, while his companion's are more directly influenced by her organism ... we have no reason to suppose that woman may ever be able to fulfill the same functions in society as man; but she will be able to play a part in society which, while peculiarly her own, may yet be more active and important than that of today [89]

4. *Sociologists cannot hope to explain anything without moving from quantitative data and the physical world into the qualitative realm of actors' subjective perceptions*

In his study of suicide Durkheim tries to avoid any reference to meanings and motives, even in studying such a personal act as this. He writes:

> Disregarding the individual as such, his motives and his ideas, we should seek directly the states of the various social environments ... in terms of which the variations of suicide occur

The state of society is the cause of suicide, individual consciousness only reflects that state. Thus:

> We must then investigate this state without wasting time on its distant repercussions in the consciousness of individuals [90]

In *The Rules of Sociological Method* Durkheim insists sociologists must consider social facts as *things*. A social fact is:

> every way of acting, fixed or not, capable of exercising on the individual an external constraint. *Things* include: all objects of knowledge that cannot be conceived by purely mental activity, those that require for their conception data from outside the mind, from observation and experiment [91]

In the case of *suicide,* the social facts being studied are the social conditions which lead a certain number of individuals to commit suicide.

However, as Keat and Urry point out, Durkheim is not successful in his attempt to confine his attention purely to external data even in his *definition* of suicide. Durkheim defines suicide as any case of death:

> resulting directly or indirectly from a positive or negative act of the victim himself, which he knows will produce this result [92]

Keat and Urry comment that Durkheim tries to avoid reference to any *intention* to commit suicide in the actor's mind. This would be an unobservable, subjective state, not an external social fact. Durkheim does use the verb 'to know' in the definition of suicide, though. So:

> Durkheim's own definition of suicide does not entirely eliminate the unperceivable, since it makes use of the concept of knowledge: this necessarily involves the concept of belief, and a belief is, in principle, no more external and perceivable than is purpose or intention [93]

Similarly his explanation of the individual's response to being in a situation of too low or too high social integration, anomie, requires empathy with him or her in order to fully understand how such a situation might lead to suicide.

In explaining suicide Durkheim attempts to avoid any reference to motives, referring instead to correlations between sets of data; the suicide statistics of different social groups. This means that we are left to conjecture on the reasons for the correlations. A number of alternative reasons are equally plausible. J Jacobs notes that although the Catholic, Protestant and Jewish religions all forbid suicide, they have a very different moral evaluation of it. He argues, after examining the *motives* for suicide by studying suicide notes, that the suicide rates for Protestants (high) Catholics (lower) and Jews (lowest) can be explained in the following way:

(a) Comparing the beliefs taught by Christianity to Judaism, Christianity promises rewards in the hereafter, Judism does not. Christians represent their deaths as 'going to heaven', Jews do not. What encourages potential Christian suicides is their ability to convince themselves of ending an intolerable life below and obtaining a better one in the beyond.

(b) Therefore, on these grounds, Jews will have a lower suicide rate than Christians whether Catholic or Protestant.

(c) Protestantism is more rationalistic than Catholicism, and stresses the ability of the individual to work out his own balance sheet of salvation. Catholicism lays greater stress on the supremacy of the dogma.

(d) Therefore, Protestants wil find it easier to construct a justification of their suicide than will Catholics who are more constrained by the *dogmatic* prohibition of suicide.

(e) Therefore, Protestants will commit suicide more than Catholics [94]

Action theorists argue that we *must* use hermeneutics, as has been done by Jacobs, to fully explain behaviour. The table summarises the criticisms of the naturalists' position from the action theorists' viewpoint. The problem with adopting the method of hermeneutics is

Summary statement of central assumptions and criticisms of naturalism

Naturalist Assumptions	Criticisms
Social phenomena have an existence external to the individuals who make up a society or social group and can thus be viewed as objective facts in much the same way as natural facts . . .	Social phenomena are of an essentially different order to natural ones owing to their symbolic nature and the subjective interpretations of social meaning by individuals in a society . . .
hence An observer can identify social facts relatively easily and objectively . . .	hence Identifying social phenomena is a very problematic exercise which involves the assumption that an action has a single unchanging meaning for all people, times and situations . . .
hence Numerical and other 'scientific' techniques can be adapted to 'measure' social facts . . .	hence Attempts to 'measure' will gloss over the above problems and lead the imposition of observers' definitions on to a situation where the extent to which these are shared by actors under study is unknown . . .
hence Hypotheses relating to measurable variables can be tested . . .	hence To construct hypotheses is to assume that the problems listed above are either trivial or have been overcome . . .
hence Social theories can be constructed on the basis of discovered 'relationships' or tested by deducing testable hypotheses from some general theoretical statement . . .	hence The attempt to explain social phenomena without reference to actors' motives and meanings misrepresents the nature of social reality . . .
hence Sociology can proceed with methodologies based on natural science models.	hence Sociology must develop alternative methodologies appropriate for studying subject matter which poses problems not faced by the subject matter of the natural sciences.[95]

that of validating one's own interpretation of action. How can we be sure, for example, that Jacob's interpretation is the correct one?

The strong form of anti-naturalism argues that social facts do not exist at all. This stance clearly rejects the objectivism of the natural sciences and the naturalists' conception of the human individual as homo sociologicus. Given that social reality is merely the construction of the individuals who compose a given social group it becomes impossible for the sociologist to explain it in any sense. It would be arrogance and folly for the researcher to believe that he/she had discovered something about the social world people live in other than that which they know. There are no laws, no real causes, only a socially created set of meanings shared by a social group. The task of the researcher can only be to explore and describe one version of reality for the benefit of those of us who do not share it.

This is the ethnographic method which literally means describing a culture. Durkheim's attempt to be a detached observer, able to explain events not properly understood by those involved (including their own deaths) cannot hope to succeed. An ethnographic approach would merely record the event from the actor's point of view. Jack Douglas does this, arguing that suicide may be:

(a) A means of release from the pressures of this world to a situation of peace and rest, even heaven.
(b) A way of making a point about oneself to others: to show that I did really love you, I am sincere, I'm not like that, I'm sorry etc.
(c) A plea for help (often failed suicides). These tend to be young, married females suffering temporary mental disorder whereas actual suicide victims tend to be old, divorced/bereaved, male, suffering long term mental illness or alcoholism.
(d) A way of getting revenge, forcing others to blame themselves for the death. This is often associated with a note, identifying who is to blame.[96]

This approach clearly implies a very different set of methodological techniques to be used to fully understand the feelings and motives of the person involved. Those on the right of the table on page 52 are best for this, those on the left do not allow access to the world of meanings of the actor.

Attempts to obtain valid results from representative samples or to compare social groups are founded on a misguided conception of social reality. Every social situation is unique, the product of its participants' interactions. Not only that but social reality is in constant flux as interaction is dynamic. Questionnaires, statistics and so on can only provide a snapshot of the social world whereas participant observation, for example, permits understanding of the social *process*. Uncontrolled experiments can provide useful insights without pretensions to reliability. For phenomenologists, especially, the sociologists' job is description and empathetic understanding, not high-flown explanation. This task can only be performed satisfactorily with depth interviews, questionnaires that allow full expression of views, life histories, the use of personal documents, uncontrolled experiments and participant observation.

5. *Sociologists cannot establish laws because of the unpredictability of human beings and the transitory nature of social reality*

The structuralist views the individual's behaviour as governed by external forces. Social roles are seen as constraining action which is conducted within social institutions which are merely organised sets of roles. Behaviour is seen as regular and predictable. Law-like statements can be made about social behaviour in just the same way as about physical phenomena. Most structuralists recognise that irregularities *do* occur in the social world and that predictions are never 100 per cent accurate. As a result probabilistic statements must be made when predicting future behaviour.

Action theorists reject probabilistic statements. Peter Winch makes the point that regularities in society are *not* the same as mechanical regularities. In order to say 'every time A happens, B follows' we need to investigate a large number of As and Bs. We have to identify a number of social events as being of the same type. To do this, we need to *understand* the nature of social behaviour, the common sense meanings of the actors themselves. The identification of regularities to establish laws implies the use of (unscientific) hermeneutics or alternatively, to quote Winch 'the imposition of one's own understanding of social reality'. For example, to study a number of cases of suicide and of social integration, Durkheim had to assume that suicide for the Protestant was the same as suicide for the Catholic (which Jacobs argues it is *not*.) He also had to estimate levels of social integration in the groups he studied. He did this by imposing his *own* understanding of high and low social integration. Winch sums these points up as follows:

... ideas and theories are constantly developing and changing, and ... each system of ideas, its component elements being interrelated internally, has to be understood in and for itself; the combined result of which is to make systems of ideas a very unsuitable subject for broad generalisations ... Historical explanation is not the application of generalisations and theories to particular instances;

it is the tracing of internal relations. It is like applying one's knowledge of a language in order to understand a conversation rather than like applying one's knowledge of the laws of mechanics to understand the workings of a watch[97]

Having examined the arguments which conclude that social reality and physical reality are of different orders and that the scientific method is unsuitable for sociology we will now examine whether science itself *really* meets scientific standards. Let us take each point in turn and apply it to natural science.

1. *Raw data is untrustworthy*

Just as one should treat apparently objective facts with some caution in sociology, so in natural science one should beware of naive inductivism. The following diagram illustrates the difference between *induction* and *deduction*.

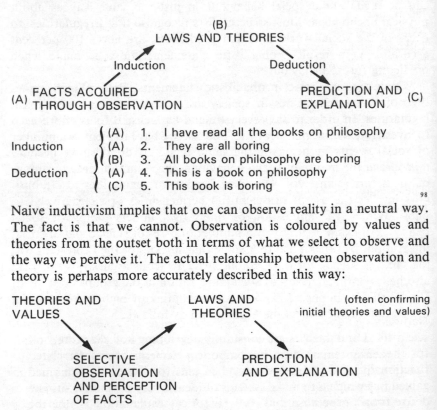

(B)
LAWS AND THEORIES

Induction   Deduction

(A) FACTS ACQUIRED   PREDICTION AND (C)
THROUGH OBSERVATION   EXPLANATION

Induction	(A)	1.	I have read all the books on philosophy
	(A)	2.	They are all boring
	(B)	3.	All books on philosophy are boring
Deduction	(A)	4.	This is a book on philosophy
	(C)	5.	This book is boring

[98]

Naive inductivism implies that one can observe reality in a neutral way. The fact is that we cannot. Observation is coloured by values and theories from the outset both in terms of what we select to observe and the way we perceive it. The actual relationship between observation and theory is perhaps more accurately described in this way:

THEORIES AND   LAWS AND   (often confirming
VALUES   THEORIES   initial theories and values)

SELECTIVE   PREDICTION
OBSERVATION   AND EXPLANATION
AND PERCEPTION
OF FACTS

The initial theories and values which the natural scientist might hold and which will colour his or her scientific work include:

1. A particular interest in the subject he/she has chosen to study.
2. A desire for experiments to succeed so that new discoveries are made.
3. The common-sense theories about the natural world which we learn in early socialisation and which are very difficult even for the natural scientist to throw off.
4. The ideas and theories which the scientist learned during training, the results of the work of other scientists.
5. The limitations imposed on objectivity by the institution within which the scientist is working.

Observation is *always* selective, no matter what its subject. It presupposes an interest, a viewpoint, a job to be done or a problem to be solved.

This description of the natural sciences, which sees them too as value-laden, may expose them to the dilemma of relativism. Their truth is no longer regarded as absolute but as relative to antecedent theories. S Lukes, a sociologist of knowledge, argues that this is not necessarily the case:

> The influences, however deep, of theories upon man's perceptions or understanding is one thing; the claim that there are no theory-independent objects of perception and understanding is another. Similarly, the influence of theories upon what men may count as valid or consistent is one thing; the claim that validity and consistency are theory-dependent is another ... [99]

There may be a number of different theories about the same phenomenon. There may be different criteria for establishing the validity of knowledge in different circumstances. Yet this does not necessarily mean that the truth or some way of discovering it once and for all does not exist.

2. *Problems with methodology*

Naturalists tend to be envious of the precise methods available to natural scientists. The controlled experiment appears to be a powerful technique for the advancement of knowledge. Karl Popper points out that the function of an experiment is only to test hypotheses, the information gained is dependent on what the experiment was set up to do. Hypotheses derive from observation and observation is structured by pre-conceived and implicit theories. Information derived from experiments is dependent upon our values and theories. It is partly for this reason that many important scientific discoveries are the result not of careful testing in controlled experiments but of accidents. Microwave cookers, photographic plates, penicillin and many other discoveries owe their existence to chance occurrences. Thomas Kuhn argues that the experimentation done in any given period of scientific work usually serves only to support the theories held at the time. Experiments which would bring about a genuine advance in knowledge are simply not thought of because the current theories do not suggest such original ones to the scientist. We can say, therefore, that while natural scientists have powerful testing techniques as their disposal, the strength of these techniques is undermined by the bias and selectivity which we have just discussed.

3. *Lack of objectivity*

Thomas Kuhn in *The Structure of Scientific Revolutions* describes in detail how the work of individual scientists may be confined to certain areas by the theories which are predominant within the scientific community at any given time. Kuhn questions the idea of science steadily building up a body of knowledge. He suggests that while this does occur for a time (the stage of *normal science*), this is interrupted by a scientific revolution. A scientist makes discoveries which convincingly demonstrate that the *axioms* (fundamental truths) of the 'old' science are flawed and need to be replaced by new ones. This period of *extraordinary science* involves conflict between the old and the new but when the new has gained the support of all scientists a fresh period of normal science commences. The build up of knowledge starts from the beginning, the old knowledge now being recognised as being wrong. Eventually another scientific revolution will occur and the battle will be played out again. Kuhn calls the set of axioms held during a period of normal science a *paradigm:*

> In chemistry ... the current paradigm is the idea that matter is composed of basic entities called atoms comprising a small central positively-charged nucleus surrounded by a diffuse, negatively-charged electron cloud. The structure of this cloud determines the way in which atoms can combine with other atoms to form molecules ... For nulcear physicists (on the other hand) ... the current paradigm is that the atomic nucleus consists of an aggregate of positively-charged particles called protons and uncharged particles called neutrons bound together by a powerful force ...
>
> ... the essential features of a paradigm are as follows:

(a) It forms the underlying theoretical model on which a particular branch or sub-branch of science is based at any given time.

(b) It is accepted without question by all ... of those working in the field at the time.

(c) It effectively determines the sort of problems that (scientists) ... should and should not investigate (no chemist, for example, would try to solve a problem solely concerned with the structure of the nucleus; such problems are the concern of ... the nuclear physicists.)

(d) It effectively determines the way in which such problems are tackled by giving rise to set procedures, rules and standards[100]

During a period of normal science the work done by scientists elaborates on the paradigm and solves problems which the paradigm throws up. Only when problems arise which cannot be answered without a radical revision of the paradigm does the possibility of a scientific revolution occur.

One example of a change of paradigm is the Darwinian revolution in the middle of the Nineteenth Century. Prior to Darwin's *On The Origin of Species* the fundamental biological paradigm was that God created all species in their present form. There was believed to be no connection between species other than a common creator. Biologists' work was seen as merely establishing taxonomies, ie classifying animals with similar characteristics into groups and sub-groups. It was the discovery of fossilised remains of now extinct animals by the new science of geology which undermined this view. These remains demonstrated slow change in physical characteristics over a period of millions of years among many different species. They also indicated the common origin of many flora and fauna, including a proposed common ancestor of man and certain apes. Darwin explained these findings by his theory of evolution through natural selection. This was opposed by both scientists and the Church but by the beginning of this century it had become the established paradigm though it is currently being questioned itself. Major paradigm shifts in other fields include the Copernican revolution (the Earth revolves around the sun, not vice versa) and the Einsteinian revolution which refuted Newton's axioms about the nature of space and time.

Kuhn's theory, if correct, implies that natural science, too, is studying not an objective but a created world, one created by the interpretations of the scientists studying it. Kuhn rejects objectivism and announces the relativism of all knowledge:

> ... paradigm changes do cause scientists to see the world of their research engagement differently. In so far as their only recourse to

that world is through what they see and do, we may want to say that after a revolution scientists are responding to a different world[101]

4. *The problem of Meaning*

Keat and Urry in *Social Theory as Science* distinguish between a variety of views of science. We will deal with positivism and realism. *Positivism* concentrates its attention on regularities of behaviour without looking into the *reasons* for the regularities. Positivists conduct experiments and replicate them until they feel sure that if X happens then Y will happen every time. They do not involve themselves in trying to develop an explanation of the observed correlation between X and Y because this will lead them into the realm of speculation and non-measurable concepts. In medicine it was discovered that one of the first symptoms of measles is the appearance of whitish spots, called Koplik spots, on the mucous linings of the cheeks. Testing suggested that this occurs in every case of measles and thus it was possible to establish a correlation without understanding the reasons for the appearance of Koplik spots.[102]

Realism, on the other hand, contends that:

> To explain phenomena is not merely to show they are instances of well-established regularities. Instead, we must discover the necessary connections between phenomena, by acquiring knowledge of the underlying structures and mechanisms at work ...

> For the realist the primary purpose of scientific theories is to enable us to give causal explanations of observable phenomena, and of the regular relations that exist between them[103]

Positivists see these causal explanations as unnecessary and unscientific. Realists point out that we know very little about the relationship between Koplik spots and measles if we adopt a purely positivist approach. Moreover we may be drawn into making the mistake of believing that the spots *cause* the measles (which they do not) or ignoring the possibility of a third factor which causes both the spots and the measles to appear.

To avoid the problems associated with establishing only *correlation,* realists will move into the realm of the non-measurable and non-observable.

One problem for the realist approach is that explanations often require explanation themselves. Realists do not know whether, eventually, one will arrive at an 'ultimate explanation' or whether in the end one simply answers the question 'why does this happen' with the response 'it just does' (a positivist reply!)

Despite these differences both positivism and realism:

> share a general conception of science as an objective rational enquiry which aims at true explanatory and predictive knowledge of an external reality[104]

The realists' qualification of positivism suggests that even natural scientists cannot limit their attention on to the outwardly observable but must explain physical behaviour sometimes by reference to non-observable and non-measurable factors. Where this is the case the scientist's explanation of phenomena is put at the same level as the action theorist's explanation of human behaviour through the hermeneutic method. Both are in the realm of non-observable, non-quantifiable phenomena.

5. *Scientific laws cannot be established*

The establishment of universally true statements of regularities in physical behaviour was considered to be one of the fundamental features of science. However David Hulme, an eighteenth century Scottish philosopher, pointed out that we can never arrive at *general* statements (laws) by conducting a finite number of *individual* observations or experiments. His argument is usually illustrated by the hypothesis 'all swans are white' (as *if* X is a swan *then* it must be white.) One could test this by observing many swans, but despite the fact that all those observed are white, the possibility remains that one day a black swan will be discovered (and indeed black swans were found to exist in Australia.) Similarly, because all known apples have always fallen to earth unless suspended does not meant that they always will do so.

This argument seemed to undermine the very foundation of the scientific approach—it meant that laws could not be established and so bodies of knowledge could not be built up. However Karl Popper,[105] while appreciating that such a statement as 'all swans are white' can never be proven, said that it can be *disproven* by the observation of a single non-white swan. He therefore recommended that theories should be tested not by attempting to prove them *right,* but by attempting to prove them *wrong.* A theory which can withstand a sustained attempt to disprove it must be considered good enough to use as a working hypothesis until a better one comes along. It is, according to Popper, impossible to establish *laws,* only workable theories. Popper's view of the scientific process looks like this:

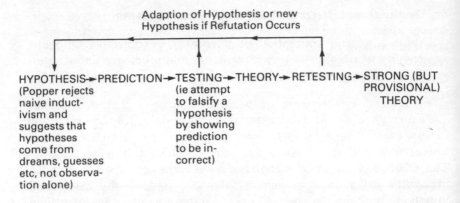

Recent discoveries about the nature of matter illustrate Popper's view of science very well.

Until quite recently it was thought that all the material in the universe was built up from a comparatively small number of fundamental particles (protons, neutrons, electrons, mesons and the neutrino). By about 1960 so many particles had been or were being discovered that all such particles could no longer be considered fundamental. An American physicist called Gell-Mann developed the *3 Quark Theory* to answer this problem. He suggested that the particles identified to date were not fundamental particles at all but were composite particles made up from three base particles known as quarks. This theory seemed to solve the problem by explaining the properties of the various particles known at the time and predicted the existence of another particle, omega minus, which was later (1964) discovered. Other predictions were also tested and found to stand up, so that Gell-Mann's theory was adopted as the basic model underlying particle physics. Some experiments produced results that did not quite fit in with the predictions of the three quark theory. This led other physicists to adapt it by suggesting the existence of a fourth quark, a charmed quark. This enabled all the discrepancies between theory and experiment to be cleared up as well as throwing up new predictions which withstood testing. The charmed quark was actually identified in 1976. In 1983 two new particles, W and Z, were discovered at the European nuclear research centre in Geneva. Their existence had been predicted by the earlier theory but further results from these experiments showed up flaws in the four quark idea. New particles, heavier than W and Z, were also discovered. According to quark theory they should not exist. Their discovery may require adaptation or even complete revision of the theory which had earlier seemed very strong.

Science too, then, is not so powerful a tool as our earlier description of it had suggested. Its knowledge is, according to some philosophers of science at least, not *the* truth but a version of the truth which may be accepted temporarily as the best available. Unlike Kuhn, Popper rejects relativism. For Popper, truth or reality does exist. While we may never completely apprehend it, it is possible for us to move nearer and nearer to it. Popper is an objectivist.

The argument that Sociology should not be Scientific

Clearly there are very good reasons for sociology not to imitate science. The action theorist proposes that physical reality and social reality are not comparable. The philosophers of science show that science is flawed in a number of ways and is not the perfect model to be emulated that it might at first appear. In addition there are a number of reasons positively to avoid naturalism. These can be summarised as follows:

1. Science is *too* rigorous. Sociology needs the open-minded creativity of the artist.
2. Science is too empirical. Sociology should be committed to change and have an ideal which it should help to attain.
3. Science is too manipulative. Sociology should *not* aim to change society (the opposite viewpoint from 2).

Let us deal with each of these points in turn.

1. Robert Nisbet writes:

    It occurred to me a number of years ago while I was engaged in exploration of some of the sources of modern sociology that none of the great themes which have provided continuing challenge and also theoretical foundation for sociologists during the last century was ever reached through anything resembling ... 'scientific method' ... The themes I refer to are ... *community, masses, power, development, progress, conflict, egalitarianism, anomie, alienation* and *disorganisation* ... What also occurred to me in my explorations was the close affinity these themes had throughout the Nineteenth Century with almost identical themes in the world of art—painting, literature, even music—and, far from least, the close affinity of the sources of motivation, inspiration and realisation of these themes[106]

Such broad themes as these are not amenable to scientific analysis. To study them requires insight, imagination and creativity. CW Mills in *The Sociological Imagination*[107] makes a similar point. He complains that social *scientists* have adopted a style of abstracted empiricism, by which he means an insight-less search for the facts. The use of rigorous methodology, closed ended questionnaires and the like has limited the areas which it is possible to study. The means have come to obscure the ends of sociological research and have become an end in themselves. Naturalists have lost sight of the greater importance of some issues over others. They have no concern for humanity or human ideals, their only concern is to maintain their objectivity. Commitment to a cause and speculation as to the reasons for observed phenomena are considered to be unscientific. We are thus left with a collection of 'facts' which, in the absence of any theory to help us make sense of them, tell us nothing.

2. A similar point is made by Marxists, but they point out the *political* implications of pure empiricism. Marx himself, like Mannheim, sees science as independent of existential determination, or relatively so. Pure science exists in the same form in any mode of production, though the problems it addresses *are* determined by the mode of production. Capitalism provides science with particular problems to solve: how to increase production or how to wage war more efficiently. Marx criticises *applied* science, not the scientific method itself. For many later Marxists, pure science is a product of capitalism. H Marcuse in *One Dimensional Man*[108] sees positivism as ideological, serving to sustain capitalism. In concentrating only on the observable it rejects a consideration of philosophical (and unobservable) concepts such as justice, democracy and fulfilment. Nicolai Bukharin agrees, arguing that positivists ignore:

> all earthly sufferings, all conflicting interests, all the ups and down of life, the hunt for profit and other earthly and vulgar things . . . (which were seen as having) . . . no relation whatever with their science[109]

because of the unmeasurable nature of these things.

This point is well illustrated by contrasting Marx's unscientific view of alienation with that of an American naturalist, Robert Blauner. For Marx alienation has four dimensions:

a. alienation from the productive activity (because the worker is unfulfilled at work in capitalism with its enslaving technology),

b. alienation from the products of work (because the articles produced belong to the owner and not the person who produced them, they give no satisfaction, indeed become an object of loathing)

c. alienation from man (because in capitalism the divisions between and within classes lead to coercion, hatred and exploitation),

d. alienation from the species being (because the proper development of society has been blocked by capitalist oppression, mankind is not properly human, the full potential of humanity has not been realised).

In Alienation and Freedom (1969) Robert Blauner attempted to make Marx's concept of alienation amenable to scientific testing. To do so he had to make it measurable. Having done so he could use questionnaires to discover whether it was present or not, and if so how much of it there was. Blauner declared that alienation was *not* present if a worker had control over work processes, was socially integrated, was involved in his/her work and had a sense of purpose in what he/she was doing. By making alienation measurable Blauner lost essential elements of Marx's vision of it. The idea of the alienation from the species being has gone, as has the notion of alienating effect of wider social relations other than those found in the work place. Marx's concept has been emasculated, its critical content removed.

For Marcuse and many other later Marxists, sociology should adopt a critical stance. Naturalists accept reality as it is. Objectivity is conservatism in this disguise. The task of sociology is to work towards social change. Though not a Marxist himself, Alvin W Gouldner in *Anti-Minotaur—the Myth of a Value-Free Sociology* agrees with the Marxist theme:

> *One* latent meaning ... of the image of a value-free sociology is this: 'Thou shalt not commit a critical or negative value judgment—especially of one's own society

By holding on to the professional ethic of objectivity sociologists can avoid rocking the boat and risk losing a university post without at the same time being regarded as cowardly or as toeing the line. Furthermore, Gouldner points out the ambiguities in the apparently simple notion of value-freedom:

> Does the belief in a value-free sociology mean that sociologists are or should be indifferent to the moral implications of their work? Does it mean that sociologists can and should make value judgments so long as they are careful to point out that these are different from 'merely' factual statements? Does it mean that sociologists cannot logically deduce values from facts? Does it mean that sociologists do not or should not have or express *feelings* for or against some of the things they study? Does it mean that sociologists may and should inform laymen about techniques useful in realizing their own ends, if they are asked to do so, but that if they are not asked to do so they should say nothing? Does it mean that sociologists should never take the initiative in asserting

that some beliefs that laymen hold, such as the belief in the inherent inferiority of certain races, are false even when known to be contradicted by the facts of their discipline? [110]

3. Science does not exist in a vacuum. The results of even the most pure science are often applied in the real world, changing that world to accord more closely with the desires of those who use the results. Thus discoveries about the structure of matter are applied in nuclear weapons and nuclear power stations. In the opinion of many people some of these applications are not beneficial for mankind, or are beneficial for only part of it.

A scientific sociology, if one were ever to be fully achieved, would be applied in the same way. We would have a sort of social technology which would be as dangerous, if not more so, as applied science. Durkheim is quite explicit about the way *his* work might be applied:

> There will emerge from our study some suggestions concerning the causes of the general contemporary maladjustment being undergone by European societies and concerning remedies which may relieve it [111]

He suggested that occupational groups, corporations, should be so structured as to replace family and community as a source of social integration. In addition marriage should be made more indissoluble, to the same end. In *The Coming Crisis of Western Sociology* Alvin Gouldner notes that functionalism in general has attempted to achieve the status of a value-free science which can solve society's problems for it. However this scientific pose masks a basic conservatism:

> Functionalism's conservatism is expressed . . . in both its reluctance to engage in social dissent or criticism and its simultaneous willingness to help solve social problems in the context of the status quo [112]

Functionalists tend to accept the concept of social problems without question. In fact a social problem is a problem for a particular group of people (see page 83). By accepting the dominant definitions of what are the social problems of a given society and attempting to solve them, functionalism is acting for that dominant group. If applied science can act against the interests of some, so can applied sociology.

Like the functionalists', much of Marx's work was intended to be scientific in nature. He established 'laws' of the development of capitalism through analysis of the facts. On the basis of this he proposed action for the improvement of the proletariat's lot.

The definition of social problems adopted here is quite different from that of the functionalist, as is the proposed solution. Marx's work shares hidden values with functionalism and biases which undermine the scientific status of the analysis and the prescription. Both perspectives offer solutions to the problems of the whole of humanity which in fact benefit only the few.

Karl Popper, in *Conjectures and Refutations* writes:

> In some of its earlier formulations (for example in Marx's analysis of the character of the 'coming social revolution') ... (Marxists') predictions were testable and in fact falsified. Yet instead of accepting the refutations the followers of Marx re-interpreted both the theory and the evidence in order to make them agree. In this way they rescued the theory from refutation; but they did so at the price of adopting a device which made it irrefutable[113]

Marx predicted that the proletariat would become increasingly pauperised under capitalism. This has not been the case; standards of living have increased over time even for the working class. Marxists have responded to the failure of this prediction by claiming that the law of pauperisation refers not to increasing *absolute* poverty but increasing *relative* poverty, the increasing gap between rich and poor. To accept the dogmatism of either functionalism *or* Marxism and to apply it would be dangerous indeed. Sociology would be in danger of becoming an ideological and practical tool for those in power to work their will on others. Perhaps we should simply accept that:

> Like it or not, and know it or not, sociologists will organise their researches in terms of their prior assumptions: the character of sociology will depend upon them and will change when they change[114]

Chapter Review

This chapter has been constructed around the themes of structuralism versus action theory and naturalism versus anti-naturalism. The debate between structuralism and action theory focuses on the nature of knowledge. The central issue is whether knowledge is produced by society and given to (or imposed on) individuals or whether it is generated by individuals themselves in a social context. Marxists and functionalists adopt the former position, phenomenologists and interactionists the latter. The debate between naturalism and anti-naturalism centres around the status of *sociological* knowlege and the related question of methodology. For naturalists, sociology should seek to emulate the scientific method as the only way of producing valid or worthwhile knowledge. For anti-naturalists, the nature of the subject matter of sociology and flaws in the scientific method itself mean that sociology should use distinct methods and generate different types of knowledge from those of the natural sciences.

These two areas of controversy are not distinct from each other. Structuralists tend to be naturalists, action theorists tend to be anti-naturalists. Structuralists like Marx and Durkheim believe that human action is not free but is constrained by the social context within which it occurs. It follows that one can establish laws and predictive statements about human behaviour by understanding the nature of the rules which govern it. These rules derive from the nature of the social structure. To understand this is to understand human action. Moreover social structures do not trouble the researcher with such inconveniences as beliefs, reasons or emotions. Social structures are not human beings and do not behave like them. Action theorists like Schutz or Blumer see the individual as free and able to act in an entirely unpredictable way. As a result it is not possible to establish laws about their behaviour. To understand them it is necessary to empathise with their reasons for action, to immerse oneself in their situation. Sociology must deal with the immeasurable, the unquantifiable and the subjective. This is precisely what natural science avoids. For the action theorist sociological knowledge is of an entirely different type from scientific knowledge. It is, however, equally valid.

Bibliography

1   K Marx and F Engels   *Selected Works*   Lawrence and Wishart, London 1973, first published 1968 p 181: Preface to   *A Contribution to the Critique of Political Economy*
2   M Mann (ed)   *The Macmillan Student Encyclopaedia of Sociology*   Macmillan, London 1983 p 223.
3   Ibid p 163 and 223.
4   Marx believes that classes have 'real' or objective interests and that these are separate from subjective ones, for example an individual's desire for promotion within a career structure. The latter are false interests, according to Marx. The real interest of the proletariat is to abolish wage labour; seeking to better oneself within the context of wage labout is an example of false consciousness. In fact this is a dubious point as Marx is putting himself in the position of final arbiter of what an individual's 'real' interests are.

5   K Marx   *The German Ideology,*   R Pascal (ed) International Publishers, New York 1947 p 39.

6   Although N Abercrombie says that the members of dominant class are more susceptible to their own ideology than the subordinate. Religious beliefs appear to have been more widespread among the bourgoisie than the proletariat in Victorian times, for example. See N Abercrombie   *Class, Structure and Knowledge*   Basil Blackwell, Oxford 1980 p 25.

7   P Hamilton   *Knowledge and Social Structure*   Routledge and Kegan Paul, London 1974 p 30.

8   K Marx and F Engels op cit 1973 p 682.

9   L Althusser   *For Marx*   Penguin, Harmondsworth 1969 p 232.

10 G A Cohen   *On Some Criticisms of Historical Materialism*   Supplementary Proceedings of the Aristotelian Society Vol 44 1970, p 138, quoted in N Abercrombie op cit p 94.

11 A Gramsci   *Prison Notebooks*   ed. and translated by Q Hoare and G N Smith, Lawrence and Wishart, London 1971 p 352.

12 B Hindess and P Q Hirst   *Pre Capitalist Modes of Production* Routledge and Kegan Paul, London 1975. This position changes in later work.

13 H Marcuse   *One Dimensional Man*   Abacus, London 1972.

14 ... 'there are spheres of thought in which it is impossible to conceive of absolute truth existing independently of the values and position of the subject and unrelated to the social context. Even a god would not formulate a proposition on historical subjects like $2 \times 2 = 4$. For what is intelligible in history (as opposed to mathematics) can be formulated only with reference to problems and conceptional constructions which themselves arise in the flux of historical experience.' K Mannheim   *Ideology and Utopia*   Routledge and Kegan Paul, London 1960 p 71. See also p 170.

15 D Harker   *One for the Money : Politics and the Popular Song* Hutchinson, London 1980.

16 D Harker op cit p 31.

17 Ibid p 34.

18 Ibid p 39 quoting I Whitcomb   *After the Ball*   Penguin, Harmondsworth 1973.

19 Ibid p 43.

20 Ibid p 47.

21 E Durkheim and M Mauss   *Primitive Classification*   Cohen and West, London 1969, first published in English 1963, in French 1903, p 88.

22 E Durkheim   *The Division of Labour in Society*   Collier

Macmillan, Toronto 1964.

23 Ibid p 79.

24 Ibid p 130.

25 Ibid p 131.

26 E Durkheim *The Elementary Forms of The Religious Life* George Allen and Unwin, London 1968 first published 1915.

27 Ibid p 9.

28 Ibid p 10.

29 R Aron *Main Currents in Sociological Thought* vol II Penguin, Harmondsworth 1970 pp 60-61, quoting E Durkheim 1968 op cit.

30 Based on E C Cuff and G C F Payne eds *Perspectives in Sociology* George Allen and Unwin, London 1982 first published 1979, p 37.

31 M Mann *The Macmillan Student Encyclopaedia of Sociology* Macmillan, London 1983 p 3.

32 K Menzies *Talcott Parsons and the Social Image of Man* Routledge and Kegan Paul, London. 1977.

33 Ibid p 99.

34 Ibid p 15.

35 Ibid p 15.

36 Ibid p 18, quoting other authors.

37 Ibid p 88.

38 Ibid p XIV.

39 N Abercrombie op cit p 133.

40 A Schutz *The Structures of the Life World* Heinemann, London 1974 p 246.

41 P Hamilton *Knowledge and Social Structure* Routledge and Kegan Paul London 1974 p 137.

42 P Berger and T Luckmann *The Social Construction of Reality* Penguin Harmondsworth 1973 first published 1966 p 78.

43 Ibid p 79.

44 Ibid p 13.

45 Ibid p 104.

46 E C Cuff and G C F Payne op cit p 135.

47 M F D Young (ed) *Knowledge and Control* Cassell and Collier Macmillan, London 1975 first published 1971 pp 5-6. Keddie's article in this volume is *Classroom Knowledge* p 133-160.

48 N Keddie (ed) *Tinker, Tailor ... The Myth of Cultural Deprivation* Penguin, Harmondsworth 1973.

49 T Gladwin *Culture and Logical Process* in Keddie ibid p 112.

50 Ibid p 113.

51 Ibid p 118.
52 For an elaboration of this and other criticisms of Young's work see G Bernbaum *Knowledge and Ideology in the Sociology of Education* Macmillan, London 1977.
53 M Sarup *Marxism and Education* Routledge and Kegan Paul, London 1978 p 4.
54. D Spender *Invisible Women : The Schooling Scandal* Writers and Readers Publishing Co-op. London 1982 p 17.
55 Quoted in P Worsley (ed) *Modern Sociology : Introductory Readings* Penguin, Harmondsworth 1970 p 44.
56 Ibid p 46.
57 This illustration is adapted from M M Poloma *Contemporary Sociological Theory* Macmillan, New York 1979 p 167.
58 H Blumer *Symbolic Interactionism : Perspective and Method* Prentice Hall, Englewood Cliffs 1969 p 5.
59 C Lacey *Hightown Grammar* Manchester University Press, Manchester 1970.
60 J Young *The Role of the Police as Amplifiers of Deviancy, Negotiators of Reality and Translators of Fantasy : Some Consequences of our Present System of Drug Control as seen in Notting Hill* in S Cohen (ed) *Images of Deviance* Penguin, Harmondsworth 1971.
61 Ibid p 30.
62 Ibid p 33.
63 D Matza *Becoming Deviant* Prentice Hall, New Jersey 1969 p 93 quoted Young ibid p 34.
64 Young ibid p 34.
65 Ibid pp 45-7.
66 I Taylor et al *The New Criminology* Routledge and Kegan Paul, London 1973.
67 The work of S Hall et al in *Policing the Crisis* Macmillan, London 1978 is an illustration of this.
68 See for example F Pearce *Crimes of the Powerful* Pluto Press, London 1978.
69 M Weber *The Protestant Ethic and the Spirit of Capitalism* Unwin University Books, London 1968.
70 P Hamilton op cit p 145.
71 R Aron op cit p 202.
72 J Gould and W L Kolb *A Dictionary of the Social Sciences* Tavistock London 1964.
73 Figures from The Annual Abstract of Statistics 1984 HMSO. International figures from New Society 8 October 1981.

74 Adapted from E Durkheim *Suicide* Routledge and Kegan Paul, London 1979 p 74. The figures for suicide and insanity refer to a variety of years, ranging from 1846 to 1861. The quotes are from p 75 and p 145 respectively.

75 From Ibid p 152.

76 Following quotes from Ibid p 209 and p 210 respectively.

77 Ibid p 239.

78 Ibid pages 252 and 253.

79 R Merton *Social Theory and Social Structure* The Free Press, New York 1949 p 370.

80 M Atkinson *Discovering Suicide : Studies in the Social Organisation of Sudden Death* Macmillan, London 1978.

81 W Stark *The Sociology of Knowledge* Routledge and Kegan Paul, London 1958 p 114.

82 Rosenthal and Jacobson *Pygmalion in the Classroom* Holt, Rinehart and Winston New York 1968.

83 E Durkheim op cit p 26 editor G Simpson.

84 The quality of the sample selected for questioning is of great importance to naturalists. They usually use some form of random sample (alternatives are simple random sample, stratified, cluster and multi-stage sampling) and try to study large numbers of people so that resulting data is statistically significant. Sampling procedures involving judgment, eg quota sampling, are avoided if possible.

85 A Oakley *Housewife* Allen Lane, London 1974, the preface.

86 A Gouldner *The Coming Crisis of Western Sociology* Heinemann, London 1972 first published 1970 in Great Britain pages 31 and 33.

87 P Trudgill *Sociolinguistics* Penguin, Harmondsworth 1974 p 25.

88 D Spender *Man Made Language* Routledge and Kegan Paul 1980 p 155-6 quoting A Graham.

89 E Durkheim op cit p 385 previous quote from p 378.

90 E Durkheim ibid p 151 and p 149.

91 E Durkheim *The Rules of Sociological Method* Collier Macmillan, Toronto 1964 p 13 and p xiii.

92 E Durkheim *Suicide* p 44.

93 R Keat and J Urry *Social Theory as Science* Routledge and Kegan Paul London 1975 p 162.

94 J Jacobs *The Use of Religion as Constructing the Moral Justification for Suicide* in J D Douglas (ed) *Deviance and Respectability : The Social Construction of Moral Meanings* Basic

Books, New York and London 1970 Quote from *Variety in Social Science Research* DE 304 Block 1, Open University Milton Keynes 1979 reprinted 1981 pp 110-111.

95 Table adapted from J M Atkinson *Discovering Suicide* Macmillan, London 1978 pp 20-21.

96 J Douglas *The Social Meanings of Suicide* Princeton University Press, Princeton New Jersey 1967.

97 P Winch *The Idea of a Social Science and its Relation to Philosophy* Routledge and Kegan Paul, London 1958 p 133.

98 The diagram and example come from A F Chalmers *What is This Thing Called Science?* Open University Press, Milton Keynes 1978.

99 S Lukes *On the Social Determination of Truth* in R Horton and R Finnegan *Modes of Thought* Faber and Faber, London 1973 p 236.

100 H Ellington *The Nature of Science* Heinemann, London p 19.

101 T Kuhn op cit quoted in S Lukes op cit p 234.

102 R Keat and J Urry op cit quoting C G Hempel *Aspects of Scientific Explanation* Free Press, New York 1965.

103 Ibid pages 5 and 32.

104 Ibid p 44.

105 K Popper *The Logic of Scientific Discovery* Hutchinson, London 1959.

106 R Nisbet *Sociology as an Art Form* Oxford University Press 1977 pp 3-4.

107 C W Mills *The Sociological Imagination* Penguin, Harmondsworth 1970 first published 1959.

108 H Marcuse *One Dimensional Man* op cit.

109 N Bukharin *Historical Materialism : a System of Society* Ann Arbor, University of Michigan Press 1969 pp 10-11.

110 A W Gouldner *Anti Minotaur : The Myth of a Value Free Sociology* in R S Denisoff *Sociology : Theories in Conflict* Wadsworth Publishing Inc Belmont California 1972 p 43 and pp 36-7.

111 E Durkheim *Suicide* op cit p 37.

112 A Gouldner *The Coming Crisis of Western Sociology* Heinemann, London 1971 p 336.

113 K Popper *Conjectures and Refutations* Routledge and Kegan Paul, London 1969 page 37 and 334.

114 A Gouldner 1971 p 28.

Glossary

Action Theory: that approach to sociology which emphasises the perceptions actors have of social situations and the motives and meanings they hold which impel them to act in certain ways.

Dialectic: the process of reconciliation of contradictions which creates a new reality. Examples from Marx's thought are: (i) the clash of proletariat and bourgeoisie to create (eventually) communist society, (ii) the dialectic between substructure and superstructure to produce changes in both.

Empirical: the opposite of theoretical. An empirical study is one based on data collected in the real world.

Epistemology: a branch of philosophy concerned with the theory of knowledge. It concerns the relationship between the perceiving subject (eg the social scientist) and the world of objects which he/she sets out to perceive and know.

Existential Determination: the determination of culture and thought by social structure or economy.

Hegemony: the dominance of certain forms of thought and ideas over others. These are accepted rather than imposed, but their continued dominance requires constant reinforcement, for example by the mass media and the education system.

Hermeneutics: refers to the process of understanding behaviour through interpreting the motives and meanings of the actor. Synonyms are verstehen and interpretive method.

Idealism: the view that ideas and individual will have the independence and power to effect changes in society. Idealism is implicit in the Great Man theory of history in many school textbooks.

Ideology: has a number of meanings from a general weltanschauung to a formal system of ideas such as fascism or Christianity. It is used by Mannheim to refer to ideas which serve to sustain the status quo. Ideology is sometimes seen as deliberately created by groups in society (a conspiracy theory) but more often as resulting in a natural way from their social situation, particularly the interests and experiences it generates.

Materialism: is the opposite of idealism. It proposes that material factors, usually the economy, predominate over other aspects of society, especially culture and knowledge. Marx's materialism suggests that the combination of technology and class structure at least influence if not determine such things as the education system, economic theories, legal and political systems etc.

Means of Production: a term used by Marx to refer to the physical things used in production. In capitalism factories are the most important. Other examples are land and tools.

Mode of Production: used by Marx to refer to a particular type of economic system. Examples are feudalism and capitalism. The mode of production results from a specific combination of means and relations of production.

Naive Inductivism: the view that observation is independent of theory.

Naturalism: the belief that the methods used by the social sciences should be the same as those of natural science. Anti-naturalists propose that social science should or must have distinctive methods.

Objectivism: is the view that a single reality exists which is amenable to description, usually by scientific methods. It is opposed to relativism.

Ontology: a branch of philosophy concerned with the nature of existence. Phenomenologists hold that 'reality' is a flimsy social creation. Functionalists see it as having a solid existence. These are two contrasting ontological positions.

Positivism: has a number of meanings. Often it simply refers to the methods used by the natural sciences. Sometimes it is used as a synonym for naturalism. This text follows Keat and Urry's usage. They use positivism to mean the explanation of observable phenomena by reference to general laws and the strict avoidance of reference to non-observable entities. Positivists are objectivists and tend to be naive inductivists.

Relationism: a word coined by K Mannheim to describe a midway position between objectivism and relativism.

Relations of Production: used by Marx to describe the relations between social classes, eg between the capialist who buys the labour offered by a 'free' worker or between a peasant tied to the lord and his land.

Relativism: the doctrine that there are no objective standards of true or false and that therefore no objectively true reality exists. Standards of truth or falsity are seen as related to the social base.

Structuralism: used here to denote the following related points: (i) the relations between the constituent elements of a structure are more important than the individual elements, and indeed that the elements themselves are composed of sets of relations. The structure thus dominates its constituent elements. (ii) regular, systematic and orderly relations exist between the elements which comprise the structure. (iii) a structure is not something that can be directly perceived by our senses. (based on R Keat & J Urry *Social Theory as Science).*

Substructure (or Infrastructure): the economic base in a particular mode of production.

Superstructure: the realm of ideas and non-economic institutions in society; educational, political, legal etc.

Verstehen: the German word for understanding. Used by Max Weber to mean empathetic understanding of the motives behind action. Used as part (only) of a full explanation of social reality—Synonym: hermeneutics.

Weltanschuung (en) (plural): the general world view held by a social group. It includes common sense concepts and taken-for-granted reality. It is seen as a product of a particular social situation and is sometimes used synonymously for ideology.

Social Policy and Administration

Definitions, Introduction and Outline of the Chapter

Peter Townsend, one of the foremost writers in the field, defines *social policy* as:

> the underlying as well as the professed rationale by which social institutions are used or brought into being to ensure social preservation or development[1]

By including the underlying as well as the professed reasons given for social policy Townsend recognises that politicians often have two sets of reasons for a particular policy: those which are stated publicly and those which are not. For example government documents on health policy during the Second World War stated that the government:

> want to ensure that in future every man and woman and child can rely on getting all the advice and treatment and care that they need in matters of personal health[2]

However an unstated aim was presumably to build up a healthy workforce and a stronger and more profitable economy.

Social administration refers to the means through which social policy is put into effect. It involves the study of such areas as care for the sick and elderly, legislation on poverty and its effects and the implementation and results of education policy. Peter Townsend argues that social policy is administered not only through bodies set up by local and national government but by industry and religious and voluntary bodies too. Students of social policy and administration should consider these areas as well as government-directed measures.[3]

Social policy and administration are often thought of as being directed at solving social problems. Townsend quite deliberately does not refer to these in his definition. This is because the concept involves a number of difficulties. For example, in many cases everyone can agree that a thing is a social problem. Hunger and disease come into this category. They affect everyone, or could do, and are considered by everyone to be bad. Other conditions may be a problem for some groups in society but not for others. This may be due to different *interests* or different *values*. An example of the former would be unemployment. For the working class it is a social problem because it entails poverty, social isolation and loss of status. To the employers it may be seen as beneficial. High levels of unemployment mean a large pool of labour from which to draw if necessary. Fear of joining the unemployed may also make unions and workers less likely to demand high wages or become involved in industrial action. Conflicting interests of employees and employers give them different views of social problems. Examples of conceptions of social problems stemming from *values* are homosexuality and increasing rates of divorce or abortion. These are considered to be problems precisely because they are thought of as wrong. At least, they are regarded as such by *some* social groups. Clearly some groups have more power than others to make their views on the current social problems the ones that are generally accepted in society.[4]

Sociologists in their research must beware of adopting the dominant conceptions of social problems. Sociology would become the instrument of the dominant group or groups, its job being to study (and hence help to solve) *their* problems.[5] Sociologists should look beyond this and study any social phenomena which require explanation. These are *sociological* problems and they may or may not be social problems as commonly defined. Moreover even where the latter are studied the sociologist must be wary of accepting the 'usual' attitudes towards them. As we saw in the chapter on the Sociology of Knowledge, common sense is often a disguise for a partial view of reality.[6]

In this chapter, we will first give a brief summary of the historical development of the welfare state. We will focus on the five 'giants' which William Beveridge attacked in his famous report on *Social Insurance and Allied Services* of 1942. They are want, disease, ignorance, squalor and idleness (unemployment). This will give an insight into the changing perceptions of governments of the aims of social policy and how to best put them into effect. It will also give a fuller understanding of the present day organisation and working of the welfare services. Looking at the social problems identified by a major government document such as the Beveridge report will clarify some of the issues just discussed.

In the next section four theoretical perspectives on social policy are described. They are the Social Democratic, Market Liberal, Marxist and Functionalist ones. The Social Democratic approach refers to a socio-political perspective rather than to the British political party of the same name. The first two perspectives adopt an individualist approach, stressing that social change is subject to human will, as expressed in social policy.[7] The latter two adopt a more structuralist stance. They see social policy as largely shaped by the requirements of the whole social system and therefore not particularly subject to human wishes.

This section is followed by a review of the effects of British social policy on each of the five giants, with an assessment of these effects from each of the perspectives. The impact of welfare reforms on inequality in society is also considered.

The final section discusses the link between sociology and social policy. The role of sociology in assisting policy makers is returned to and elaborated on. The question of the choice of research area which the sociologist has to make and the attitudes the individual adopts towards the research are explored.

The Nature and History of the Welfare State

A welfare state is:

> a state in which organised power is deliberately used (through politics and administration) in an effort to modify the play of market forces in at least three directions—first, by guaranteeing individuals and families a minimum income irrespective of the market value of their work or their property; second, by narrowing the extent of 'social contingencies' (for example, sickness, old age and unemployment) which lead otherwise to individual and family crises; and third by ensuring that all citizens without distinction of status or class are offered the best standards available in relation to a certain agreed range of social services. [8]

Many people consider the welfare state in Britain began on 5 July 1948. This was the appointed day for its commencement as decreed by the National Insurance Act of 1946, the NHS Act of 1946 and the National Assistance Act of 1948. This view is wrong because there were elements of a welfare state as far back as the early seventeenth century. It is also wrong because we have not yet fully achieved a welfare state. Many people still live *below* the minimum decreed standards.

In his report on Social Insurance and Allied Services 1942 [9] which set out the plan for a post war system of comprehensive insurance for British citizens, William Beveridge wrote:

> There are some who will say that pursuit of security as defined in this Report, that is to say income security, is a wholly inadequate aim. Their view is not merely admitted but asserted in the Report itself. The Plan for Social Security is put forward as part of a general programme of social policy. It is one part only of an attack upon five giant evils: upon the physical Want with which it is directly concerned, upon Disease which often causes the Want and

brings many other troubles in its train, upon Ignorance which no democracy can afford among its citizens, upon the Squalor which arises mainly through haphazard distribution of industry and population, and upon the Idleness which destroys wealth and corrupts men, whether they are well fed or not, when they are idle. In seeking security not merely against physical want, but against all these evils in all their forms, and in showing that security can be combined with freedom and enterprise and responsibility of the individual for his own life, the British community and those who in other lands have inherited the British tradition have a vital service to render to human progress.

The welfare state should protect its citizens from the five giant evils, it was agreed.

Perhaps the easiest way to describe the development of the welfare state in Britain is to follow Beveridge's lead and deal with each of the five giants in turn, while remembering that this is only an analytical device. In reality they are *not* separate, as the presence of one can lead to the others.[10]

Want

The Poor Law Acts of 1601 made each parish officially responsible for its poor. A poor rate was established (a local tax to provide poor relief) and work was found for the unemployed. The poor were helped in their own homes where possible. There were also punitive houses of correction, 'Bridewells', which had existed previously and which became more evident over time. The name had terrible associations of starvation and cruelty in many people's minds.

The Speenhamland System, adopted in the 1790's in Berkshire was a humane approach to dealing with the poor. Low wages were supplemented by the parish according to a formula based on the size of a worker's family and the price of bread. By 1818 this system was used in all southern English Counties and parts of the Midlands. By 1832 the total poor rate had reached £7m, compared with £1½m in 1775, provoking an outcry from ratepayers. At the same time farmers knew they could keep wages low as the parish would supplement them.

The Poor Law Amendment Act 1834 grouped parishes into unions to provide workhouses jointly. The whole system was run by a national Central Board consisting of three Commissioners. Workhouses were set up, or continued, and were often run in the tradition of the Bridewells.

No able bodied person was now eligible for outdoor relief, that is, a dole outside the workhouse. Indeed the old, the sick, the mentally ill and unmarried mothers would often find themselves in the workhouse too. The idea was to make conditions in the workhouse worse than those outside, thus discouraging deliberate scrounging. Workhouses lasted until 1929 when the Boards of Guardians, administering the Poor Law, were abolished and replaced by the Public Assistance Committees of local authorities. The Poor Law itself was abolished in 1948. The tension between the relative generosity of the Speenhamland System and the punitive nature of welfare under the Poor Law Reform Act continues in different guises today.

The Old Age Pension Act of 1908 set up a means-tested, non-contributory pension payable to those over 70 years of age. The National Insurance Act 1911 set up a system in which employees, government and employers each paid weekly contributions to insure workers, giving them the benefit of an income and free doctor's services during times of sickness and unemployment. There was a time limit on the benefits available, but often the government would permit claimaints to be paid after this had expired. In 1931 the Goverment reduced benefits and introduced a means test for those claiming after their limit had expired. This provoked considerable opposition. Partly as a result of this the Unemployment Assistance Board (UAB) was set up in 1934 paying out assistance to those who were not, or no longer, insured. This was a means-tested payment. In1940 the UAB was renamed the Assistance Board which by now had replaced the Public Assistance Committees. In 1925 the Widows, Orphans and Old Age Contributory Pensions Act extended the range of those eligible for pensions and made more of them contributory.

The 1944 and 1946 National Insurance Acts set up a comprehensive scheme of flat-rate insurance contributions with benefits covering sickness, unemployment, old age pension, injuries, death, maternity and widow's and guardian's entitlements. These were amended by the 1959 National Insurance Act. Instead of just a flat rate contribution there was now an additional income related contribution (4.5 per cent of all income within certain limits.) Pensions were earnings-related in return, but less than the value of the contributions. This principle was extended under the National Insurance Act 1966, introducing earnings-related contributions and benefits for unemployment, sickness and widowhood.

The Family Allowances Act 1945 provided a payment to families for each child after the first up to school-leaving age. This was replaced by the 1975 Child Benefit Act (operational in 1977) which gave an untaxed benefit for all children, including the first. Tax allowances for children were phased out after 1977.

The National Assistance Act 1948 set up the National Assistance board (replacing the Assistance Board) to give assistance to the uninsured or inadequately insured. This was means tested and is the non-contributory benefit we now call (since 1966) supplementary benefit.

The Family Income Supplement Act 1970 introduced family income supplement for the working parent(s) on a low income. It is means-tested and provides a supplement to earnings for those families who, though earning, have an income below a level prescribed by the Government. Such families are not eligible for supplementary benefit precisely because they *are* working. Under other benefits a 'wage-stop' operated, meaning that a claimant could not receive more from the Department of Health and Social Security (DHSS) than he/she would have normally received from being employed. Heavily criticised for putting poor families into a poverty trap simply to discourage scrounging, the wage-stop was abolished for claimants of supplementary benefit in 1974.

The Social Security and Social Security (Pensions) Acts of 1975 aimed to rationalise the insurance scheme set up under the 1944, 1946, 1959 and 1966 Acts. The existing pension arrangements were integrated and broadened and mechanisms were established for keeping them in line with earnings and prices (though in 1981 they became linked only to prices, not earnings.) National insurance contributions for all employed people became earnings-related, the flat rate element being abolished.

The Social Security Act 1980 abolished the Supplementary Benefits Commission which had an advisory function and could exercise discretionary powers in certain cases. The Act made the supplementary benefit system much less flexible than it had been, laying down rigid rules for special payments to claimaints. Changes were also made to the rates of supplementary benefit paid to long-term claimaints. Workers on strike had some of their rights to supplementary benefit withdrawn.

In January 1982 the earnings-related supplements paid in cases of sickness, unemployment and widows allowance benefits were abolished. A flat rate again became payable (though contributions are still earnings-related.)

On the 5th July 1982 unemployment benefit and supplementary benefit paid to the registered unemployed became taxable. This has been heavily criticised for bringing the poor into the net of taxation and helping to create a poverty trap which makes it very difficult for the under-privileged to escape their circumstances.

Disease
The Public Health Act 1848 set up local boards of health where the death rate was above average. A General Board of Health was also set up but lasted only ten years.

The Medical Act of 1858 established the medical register of doctors so that the standards of their qualifications come up to a minimum level.

The Sanitary Act of 1866 compelled local authorities to appoint sanitary inspectors who could take action over questions of water supply and sewage disposal.

The 1875 Public Health Act established local health authorities in every area, under the control of a medical officer of health. A new government department, the Local Government Board, had been created in 1871 to be the central body responsible for health and the Poor Law in the country.

In 1902 the Midwives Act ensured that midwives, like doctors, are properly qualified.

The Education Act of 1907 provided for the medical inspection of school children in elementary schools. In 1914 school meals had to be provided. Under the 1918 Education Act local authorities had to provide facilities for the medical treatment of school children.

In 1929 the responsibility for the administration of the Poor Law was taken over by the local authorities who became responsible for the hospitals run under that law.

The National Health Service Act 1946 nationalised all hospitals (both ex-Poor Law and voluntary) and put them under the control of regional hospital boards. Some teaching hospitals remained outside this system.

In 1958 The Disabled Persons (Employment) Act enabled local authorities to provide work for disabled people.

The 1959 Mental Health Act amended by the 1982 Mental Health (Amendment) Act had the underlying principle that mentally disordered people should be treated, as far as possible, in the same way as those who are physically ill.[11] The idea was that the mentally ill should no longer be stigmatised or treated as second class NHS patients. Increasingly the mentally ill and handicapped are being taken out of special institutions and put either into *general* hospitals or the community. The Health and Social Services and Social Security Adjudication Act 1982 established financial provision to enable the mentally handicapped to leave hospital and live in the community.

The Local Authorities Social Services Act 1970 set up Social Service Departments in local authorities. This made it statutory to put under one department the work previously done by several. Their work is dealt with in more detail below.

The Chronically Sick and Disabled Persons Act 1970 aimed at identifying the disabled and drawing them into the welfare state. It also made provision for special facilities for them. Examples of this are adapting public premises for wheelchairs, giving local authorities the duty to provide practical assistance in the home and recreational facilities and providing for the special housing needs of the chronically sick and disabled.

The NHS Reorganisation Act 1973 (operational in 1974) changed the administrative structure of the NHS. The aim was to unify the system which had previously been divided into the Hospital Service, the General Medical, Dental, Pharmaceutical and Ophthalmic Service and the Community Service. Administration was carried out by Regional Hospital Boards (and Boards of Governors), Executive Councils and the Local Authorities.

The Health and Safety at Work Act 1974 made health and safety at work the responsibility of a Health and Safety Commission which was answerable to Parliament. Employers and unions were also given responsibilities for health and safety under this Act.

The Health Services Act 1980 once again changed the structure of the NHS, the changes to be implemented over two or three years. New local bodies, called District Health Authorities, replaced the old local bodies and the middle level of management. The latter had come under much criticism for being a redundant layer of bureaucracy.

Let us now examine in more detail the services and benefits available for the disabled and in the community.

1. *Local Authority Social Services Departments*

Social services departments are concerned, among other things, with the personal social services. These include the provision of residential care for children, the elderly and the mentally handicapped and the activities of non-residential social workers. The diagram (on page 91) illustrates the organisation of a typical department.

2. *Community Health Services*

Home nursing for the bedridden, elderly and chronically sick
Health visiting for expectant mothers
Maternity and child welfare clinics
Family planning services
Midwifery for mothers confined at home
Ambulance service
Care and after-care
Vaccination and immunisation services
Health centres which can provide a range of medical services in one place; dental, ophthalmic and pharmaceutical as well as GP's.

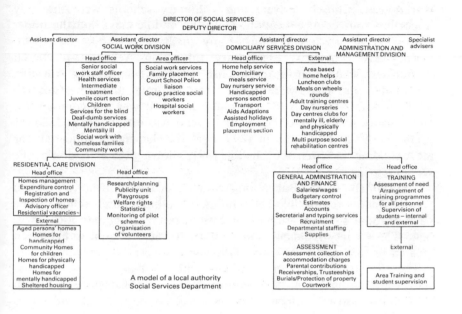

A model of a local authority Social Services Department
SOURCE: J Mays et al (eds) *Penelope Hall's Social Services of England & Wales,* RKP, 1983 p 221.

3. *Benefits for the Disabled*

Attendance allowance, for those so severely disabled that they require night and day supervision.

Invalidity pension, for the sick and disabled who do not qualify for benefit under the national insurance scheme. Mobility allowance, which helps to pay transport costs for those unable, or almost unable, to walk. This was introduced in 1976 and replaced the three-wheeled car (much criticised as unsafe.)

Invalid care allowance is paid to those looking after a disabled person who is in receipt of the attendance allowance.

Ignorance

Prior to 1870 the State's role in education was limited to the provision of grants to some church schools, some teacher training responsibility, and the education of pauper children in schools associated with some workhouses. Church, private and voluntary schools were the only important sources of education. Only the middle class and the upper class could afford an education of any quality.

The 1870 (Forster's) Elementary Education Act set up elected authorities, School Boards, to establish schools where existing provision was inadequate. These were funded from the rates and education was made available for 5 to 13 year olds, though it was not compulsory. Compulsory education to the age of 10 years was introduced in 1880, 11 years in 1893 and 12 years in 1899. Fees for elementary education for most children had been abolished in 1891, allowing the extension of the school leaving age.

The 1902 (Balfour's) Education Act made local authorities rather than School Boards responsible for schools, including church schools. The basis of today's organisation of education, run by local authorities, was laid. The County Councils and County Borough Councils had been created in 1888 under the Local Government Act.

The 1918 Education Act raised the school leaving age to 14 years. Increasing national control of education was established, with central government also accepting more of the burden of cost. Local Authorities had now to report to a central Board of Education.

In 1944 (Butler's) Education Act was based on three earlier reports. The Hadow Report of 1926 recommended a school leaving age of 15 years, selective secondary education beginning at 11 years and parity of esteem—equal status—for different types of school. The Spens report of 1938 recommended a diversification of types of secondary schools and the 1943 Norwood Report recommended the tripartite system. The Act ensured compulsory and free state education from 5 to 15 years, set up the primary (5-11 years), secondary (11-15 years) and further (16-18 +) schools and colleges. It also marked the introduction of the tripartite system of education: the grammar, secondary modern and secondary technical schools, though few of the latter were built. There was to be parity of esteem and easy transfer between the three types of schools, though neither goal was achieved. The selection process, the 11 + examination, was later shown to be inefficient and biased towards the middle class.

Four post war reports were very critical of the education system of the time. The 1959 Crowther Report *(Fifteen to Eighteen)* pointed out that most 15-18 year olds received no formal education despite the expansion of courses in further education and technical colleges. The 1963 Robbins Report on Higher Education recommended the expansion of higher education so that places were available for those who wanted them and were qualified for them. It was felt that talent and potential were being wasted through the absence of facilities to develop them. The 1963 Newsom Report *(Half Our Future)* found that 80 per cent of schools attended by average and below average ability students were deficient in terms of accommodation. These were mainly secondary modern schools. Finally the 1967 Plowden Report *(Children and Their Primary Schools)* pointed out the deficiencies in schools in poorer areas. These included noisy environments, high staff turnover, inadequate facilities and large class sizes. The Report recommended positive discrimination for schools in deprived areas, which would be termed Educational Priority Areas. Extra money was made available for better staff-pupil ratios and facilities. Suggestions were also made to improve school management, to abolish coporal punishment and to appoint specialists to look into the particular problem these schools had.

The election of a Labour government under PM Wilson in 1964 marked a turn in central government's attitude towards the tripartite system. Favouring comprehensivisation, the Ministry of Education issued Circular 10/65 asking all local education authorities to submit plans for a reorganisation of the tripartite into a comprehensive system. This is a system of non-selective schools which accept all children from their catchment area. Already in 1962 one in ten secondary school pupils were in comprehensive or near comprehensive schools. In 1964 71 per cent of all LEAs had or intended to have some form of comprehensivisation in their area. Circular 10/65 was consolidating a trend which had begun locally in the 1950's. By 1982 well over 80 per cent of secondary school pupils were in comprehensive schools. This was despite the Conservative Party's hostility to comprehensives and their issuing of Circular 10/70 recommending the re-establishment of selectivity upon being elected to government in 1970. In 1974 a Labour government returned and their 1976 Education Act *imposed* a non-selective system on all LEAs (though some refused to implement it.) This was repealed by the 1979 Education Act, introduced by the new Conservative government.

The Education System today

Since 1972 the school leaving age has been 16 years, with 5 years being the latest age at which children start school. State nursery education is available for children under 5 years in many areas, but since 1976 the number of schools and classes for the under 5's has decreased and the Education Act of 1980 removed the obligation from LEAs to provide nursery education. 1980 also saw the introduction of an element of selectivity by making provision for Assisted Places at non-state schools. This means that means-tested grants were made available for able pupils to enable them to enter the private sector. £70m was set aside to fund these Assisted Places. In some areas the age-range structure of schools has changed, some are Infant only (5-7 years), or Junior only (7 + years), some areas have Middle schools (8-12, 9-13 or sometimes 10-13 years.) Some have secondary schools with sixth forms, others are developing tertiary sectors so that pupils attend a school or college which deals only with post 16 year olds. Most LEAs retain the comprehensive system in some form despite the 1979 Act.

Despite Labour Party opposition, a variety of non-state sector schools still exist for those who can afford to attend them or who win Assisted Places or scholarships. Independent schools (or Public Schools) are exclusive in their intake. Many are grant-aided in some way by the government and they have charitable status. Direct Grant schools were private schools which received a per capita grant in return for giving at least 25 per cent of their places from state primary schools, the LEA then paying the fees for these pupils. This system raised many objections and they began to be phased out in 1977. Voluntary schools are the property of voluntary bodies, usually the Church of England or the Roman Catholic Church. About half of them are controlled schools which means that the LEA accepts certain financial liabilities in return for some control over the administration and standards in the school. Polytechnics, colleges of higher education and further education and technical colleges are funded and controlled by LEAs. The colleges of further education are now increasingly dealing with courses associated with the Manpower Services Commission's Youth Training Scheme. The universities are independent, though they receive grants from central government through the University Grants Commission. They award their own degrees. Local education authorities have a responsibility to give special provision for the education of the handicapped. Some attend ordinary schools, others go to special schools, depending on the nature and degree of their handicap. Most of these are day schools.

Squalor

Housing is usually the costliest single item of expenditure in a family's budget. Poor housing can lead to other social problems, while insanitary conditions lead to the spread of disease. Concern for the health hazards associated with poor housing was the prime motivation for the earliest legislation on this aspect of the welfare state.

94

(i) *Early legislation*

The 1868 Artisans' and Labourers' Dwellings Act empowered the medical officer of health to declare houses unfit for human habitation and to compel owners to improve or demolish the house. The 1875 Public Health Act allowed local authorities to lay down statutory minimum standards for new housing. These powers were strengthened by the 1890 Housing Act which additionally *compelled* local authorities to act where insanitary propery existed within their area. The building of 'council houses' for rent was permitted under this Act (extending the powers to do so granted by an Act of 1851) but few authorities did so. The 1909 Town Planning Act saw local authorities begin to take responsibility for the planning of their areas by permitting them to prepare schemes for the development of land.

(ii) *Subsidised council house building and rents*

Although local authorities were empowered to build houses for rent, the costs of doing so were so prohibitive that few could build them. The 1919 Housing and Town Planning Act (with powers extended by a similar Act in 1932) tried to solve this by subsidising local authorities' house building from central government funds, also permitting the houses to be let below an economic rent. The twin questions of whether central government should subsidise council house building and of uneconomic rents for their tenants were something of a political football, kicked between the Labour and Conservative Parties when each achieved office between 1919 and the present day. Subsidies on building are disliked by Conservative governments because:
(a) they are costly,
(b) they artificially lower the price and expand demand for houses,
(c) they are unfair because all authorities receive subsidies regardless of their housing problems and circumstances. Some tenants can receive subsidised housing even though they could afford to pay an economic rent.

The Labour Party tend to argue that the problems of housing shortage, poor quality housing and deteriorating neighbourhoods can only be effectively solved by central government subsidies and low rents. Subsidies were abolished in 1933 under the Housing (Financial Provisions) Act but were partially restored in 1935 and more fully by the post war Labour government (in 1946.) The 1950's saw a large number of council houses built and occupied, though subsidised rents were abolished by the Conservatives' 1957 Housing Act. They were re-introduced in 1965 (by Labour's Rent Act) which also set up rent tribunals to establish fair rent levels in industrial areas. People living in houses in poor condition became entitled to a reduced rent under the 1968 Rent Act. When the Conservatives returned to power they passed the Housing Finance Act, 1972, which:

(a) withdrew subsidies for council house building,
(b) set council rents at an economic level,
(c) enabled poor tenants to claim rent rebates,
(d) enabled selective subsidies to be paid to Local authorities with particularly bad housing problems.

However, Labour's 1975 Housing, Rents and Subsidies Act:

(a) re-introduced general subsidies for house building,
(b) allowed local authorities to determine their own rent levels,
(c) continued the rent rebate scheme.

The 1980 Housing Act cut the subsidies available for house building, while limits on the rate-support grant (block grant) from central to local government meant that authorities have built fewer houses and have had to charge economic rents. Councils spending above limits set by central government (including spending on housing) have been 'fined', they receive a lower grant in the following year. As a result of all this rents for council houses rose by 20 per cent in the first two years of the Conservative government's office. [12]

(iii) *Other post-war housing measures*

The 1946 New Towns Act (consolidated by similar Acts in 1965 and 1968) provided for the building and administration of new towns to cater for the populations of deteriorating inner city areas such as those of London and Liverpool. The aim was to provide pleasant socially mixed towns which would also become centres of industry through the provision of facilities and financial incentive for companies to move or set up there. Examples are Crawley, Harlow, Cumbernauld, Skelmersdale, Corby and Milton Keynes. In 1976, though, it was decided to transfer resources from New Towns to inner cities.

The 1947 Town and Country Planning Act made the approval of all land development by local authorities obligatory. This was amended by the 1968 Planning Act which widened the extent of local authorities' obligations in this respect. It also included provision for public participation in planning.

The 1949 Housing Act permitted grants to be paid to householders by local authorities to help them improve their homes in certain specified ways. New legislation is planned for 1985 which will means-test these grants, which are currently given for houses below a certain rateable value regardless of the owner's income. In 1981, £129 million was spent on these grants, the 1983-4 figure being in the region of £900 million. Young professional and business couples, often on above average incomes, have proved particularly adept at finding types of house that can get the maximum discretionary grant. [13]

The 1957 Housing Act permits local authorities to build, convert, acquire, enlarge or improve property to meet housing need. The Housing Acts of 1969 and 1974 empowered local authorities to designate areas needing improvements in housing and allows them to make grants and compel landlords to renovate if necessary. The 1977 Housing (Homeless Persons) Act imposes obligations on local authorities to provide temporary accommodation for persons in urgent need of it, as long as that need could not have been forseen. This was the first time such a duty had been imposed, and the Act has been applauded by its supporters for this and for giving the responsibility to housing departments (which have the real power in this respect) rather than social services departments. However many councils have adopted a strict interpretation of the clause which absolves them of obligations in cases of foreseeable homelessness. The excessive use of private hotels, often unsupervised by local government, to provide temporary accommodation has also led to complaints that unscrupulous hotel owners and private landlords are profiting by providing substandard accommodation at excessive cost.

One of the problems facing governments where rented accommodation is concerned is whether to protect tenancies or not. Clearly it is undesirable that a landlord should have the power to deprive a tenant of a home for purely personal reasons or greed. On the other hand the provision of too much protection to tenants means that landlords will sell rather than rent their property and thus the stock of accommodation available to those who cannot afford to buy declines. This occurred under the 1974 Rent Act which gave protection to tenancies in furnished as well as unfurnished accommodation (protected under the 1965 Rent Act.) The 1980 Housing Act tried to bring more rented accommodation on to the market by giving some tenants only limited security of tenure for a period of between one to five years. At the same time it gave council house tenants greater security of tenure and allowed them more freedom to alter their homes. In addition it made it compulsory for local authorities to sell their properties to sitting tenants who wished to buy. The price was to be below the market value to take account of the rent paid earlier. [14]

In November 1982 and April 1983 the housing benefit scheme replaced rent and rate rebates and supplementary benefit rent payments. Some administrative chaos occurred during the transition, resulting in benefits being withheld for a period in many cases. Housing benefit is available to council and private tenants whether or not they are claiming supplementary benefit. It is a means-tested payment for those who cannot afford rent and rate payments.[15] For owner occupiers on low incomes rate rebates and tax relief are available providing their property does not exceed a certain value.

The Housing Situation Today

The following table shows the remarkable change in the nature of Britain's housing stock since 1947.

Type of Housing, Great Britain	1947	1981	1982
Owner-occupied	26%	56%	58.9%
Local authority	13%	31%	29.5%
Rented privately	61%	13%	11.6%

This demonstrates the remarkable increase in owner-occupation and corresponding decline in private tenancies. A second recent development is the vast increase in the activities of housing associations. Since 1974 they have built more and more houses; by 1978 they were producing over 20,000 a year.[16] They generally provide rented accommodation of a good standard and at a reasonable rent, being a non-profit making alternative to the private landlord. They are given local government assistance in the form of a grant for each dwelling built or improvement made, though these have recently been reduced by central government limits on the rate-support grant.

Idleness (unemployment)

Unemployment is considered one of the giant evils to be eradicated by the welfare state because on the personal level it causes poverty and is distressing to the individual in that it can cause social isolation and a feeling of worthlessness. Economically it is a waste of human resources which could be contributing to the national economy. Finally on a large scale it can lead to mass discontent with associated political reper- cussions, even revolution. The causes of unemployment are numerous. Many jobs, particularly those associated with agriculture and holidays, are seasonal. In the off-season, normally winter, there will be temporary unemployment. Unemployment results from a mis-match between the type of work available and the skills of those looking for work. There may also be a geographical mis-match, jobs are available in one place and the unemployed are located in another. So-called 'frictional' unemployment is the result of a number of people changing jobs but being temporarily unemployed between them. More serious and longer-term unemployment may result from

(a) economic depressions, in which there is a lack of demand for products and so companies have to shed labour,
(b) structural unemployment, in which a country's key industries decline. This may result from foreign competition, changes in demand for products or the invention of new products which reduce demand for the old,
(c) technological unemployment, in which production processes are mechanised or automated, resulting in a reduced workforce.

Early measures to prevent unemployment

The 1905 Unemployed Workmen Act was the first attempt to deal with this problem on a national scale. It empowered local authorities to add to the voluntary resources available for helping the unemployed. This contribution was paid for by a halfpenny, or sometimes penny, rate. Distress Committees could look into cases of need and provide work, set up labour exchanges and, where possible and suitable, arrange emigration. In 1906, £200,000 was voted by Parliament from Treasury funds to supplement the money raised by voluntary organisations and the rate for the relief of unemployment.

Under the 1909 Labour Exchanges Act a national system of Labour exchanges was established with William Beveridge as Director. The idea was to provide a central place where jobs available and those looking for work could be 'matched', thus helping both the employers and the unemployed. They paid out unemployment relief in cases where a job could not be found. Other pre-World War Two measures to alleviate the poverty caused by unemployment are dealt with on pages 86-87.

Post War Measures

In the Employment White Paper of 1944, William Beveridge said that he considered it impossible to *totally* eliminate unemployment; the factors causing short-term unemployment discussed above would always be present. However, he argued that the government should intervene in the working of the economy and could, through suitable measures, keep unemployment to a minimum of 3 per cent of the total workforce. Until the 1970's governments bettered this figure, using the kind of policies he proposed. We deal with government measures to tackle unemployment under the following headings:

(a) measures to preserve the demand for labour,
(b) measures to protect and preserve existing jobs,
(c) measures to 'match' jobs with the unemployed.

(a) *Measures to preserve the demand for labour*

(i) Government can create public corporations (publicly owned organisations) which have a certain amount of independence from government but are accountable to parliament and to the minister concerned. One of the aims is to save companies which might otherwise go bankrupt. In this way jobs are preserved and the demand for labour in these industries maintained. Sometimes the public corporation is given a monopoly in its sector. In this case *nationalisation* has taken place. Examples of public corporations are The National Coalboard (Coal-mining Nationalisation Act 1946), British Rail (Transport Act 1947) and Upper Clyde Shipbuilders (taken over in 1971.)

(ii) Government can assist industry with subsidies and loans without taking them over. Again, this is usually done to preserve or create jobs, either in the private sector or in publicly owned industry. Examples are subsidies to the DeLorean car company, Chrysler (at its Linwood factory in Scotland, which subsequently closed), British Rail, British Leyland.

(iii) Mrs Thatcher's government is very concerned to help small businesses survive and compete within the context of a free market. Small co-operative companies, owned and controlled by their workers are also helped by government. The hope is that by giving such companies a helping hand initially they will expand and create jobs in the longer term. The 1979-83 government started a scheme by which unemployed people with some capital are 'paid' weekly by government if they start a new business. After one year, however, they must be self-supporting. The Co-operative Development Agency was set up to give grants and advice to people setting up co-operatives. In April 1981 the Community Enterprise Programme (now called the Community Programme) was established. It paid the adult unemployed a small wage for work aimed at improving the local environment. It is financed by the Manpower Services Commission.

(iv) Government can, through manipulation of taxation, the supply of money and of tariffs on imports, regulate the demand for products in the country. This will indirectly affect the level of employment; it will increase as demand increases. It was J M Keynes, the economist, who suggested that fiscal (tax) policy should not just be orientated to the collection of money for government spending but should be an instrument in the control of the economy. Such policies should virtually eliminate unemployment, especially if combined with increased government spending on public works, Keynes argued. By reducing income and other taxes and by increasing the money supply people buy more, more products need to be produced and hence employment rises. Imposing tariffs on imports ensures that it is *British* goods they buy and hence *British* jobs they create. If continued too far these policies can 'overheat' the economy, causing inflation and other problems. They need to be judiciously applied to create a balance between unemployment and inflation (which can result from excessive demand and a large supply of money.) Such policies worked well until the 1970's when, in the context of world recession, Britain suffered from both lack of demand *and* inflation (so called stagflation.)

(v) Both Conservative and Labour governments have introduced a number of special employment measures. They include the Young Workers Scheme which provides a sum of money per week (£15 in 1983) to employers for each young person they employ at a wage below a certain figure (£40 per week in 1983.) The Job Release Scheme, set up under Labour, allows men of 64 years of age to retire one year early on favourable pension terms, the idea being that they make way for a young unemployed person to replace them. The Work Sharing Scheme is designed to split one job between two people, thus allowing each to have at least half a job. The government estimated in 1983 that well over half a million jobs had been created or maintained as a result of these and other special employment measures, though this may be optimistic.

(b) *Measures to protect and preserve jobs*

The 1964 Industrial Training Act set up industrial tribunals. These are small courts which look into cases of dismissal and fine employers where necessary. The 1974 Trade Union and Labour Relations Act ensured the right of employees to belong to trade unions and gave them protection against unfair dismissal. The 1975 Employment Protection Act gave trade unions a considerable range of rights to information and consultation, in addition to strengthening employees' rights with regard to unfair dismissal. Under the Act, trade unions can have their claims investigated by ACAS; the Advisory, Conciliation and Arbitration Service. These rights were consolidated under the 1978 Employment Protection (Consolidation) Act.

101

(c) *Measures to 'match' jobs with the unemployed*

Areas of Britain with particularly high levels of unemployment have received special help since 1934 (the Special Areas Act) which attempted to attract industry to the areas worst hit by the depression: so called depressed areas. The 1945 Distribution of Industry Act enlarged and renamed them development areas. This was amended by the 1972 Industry Act which set up three types of assisted areas which are (in order of priority): special development areas, development areas and intermediate areas. Financial assistance and help with premises is given to new industries in these places. This is paid for by central government and EEC funds. Several areas lost assisted area status in June 1982, however. The setting up of assisted areas is an attempt to move industry to the unemployed. The reverse process was aided by the Redundancy Payments Act 1965 and 1969 which entitles workers who have been with a firm for more than two years to a lump sum if they are made redundant. The idea is that the money enables the individual to find new work by moving to a new area if necessary. Adequate provision of local authority houses in areas where jobs are available (such as New Towns) is also designed to assist the unemployed in this respect.

In 1973 the employment exchanges, first set up in 1909, were given a new modern image, more central locations in towns and were renamed Jobcentres. The aim was to make them more available and attractive, thus more efficient in their task of matching jobs and people. In the early 1980's, however, many of them were closed as part of the government's attempt to reduce spending. The 1983 Conservative government is attempting to replace Jobcentres with 'serve-yourself' job areas in libraries and other public buildings.

The Employment and Training Act 1973 set up the Manpower Services Commission. It now has a staff of over 20,000, employed in three main divisions: Employment Services Division, Training Services Division and Special Programmes Division.

The first is responsible for Jobcentres, among other things. The second for training and re-training in shortage skills. This can be done in skillcentres, colleges of further education or on employers' establishments. It was also responsible for the coordination and financing of 23 Industrial Training Boards, each involved in a particular area of industry. Sixteen of these were abolished in 1981 and the rest are now financially independent. The Special Programmes Division is the one which attracts most attention. It is responsible for the current Youth Training Scheme. This provides vocational training and general education for school leavers, who receive a small sum per week and can be based either at a college or an employer's establishment. Both colleges and employers receive money from the MSC for taking on YTS trainees in return for a commitment to give them skills to make the trainees more employable at the end of their one-year scheme. [17]

This outline of legislative measures is useful because it allows us to chart many of the important developments in the welfare state and gives us an understanding of the origins of the current situation. In some ways it is misleading. This is so for two main reasons.

Firstly, historical accounts of reform such as these tend to suggest that over the years we have seen a slow but sure process of construction, a gradual improvement which has seen the central goal coming nearer and nearer into view. The truth is that there is no agreement on the nature of that goal, it changes its form over the years and with changes of government. As we shall see in the next section, it is one thing for Social Democrats, another for Market Liberals. Moreover, far from seeing a gradual improvement, with the welfare state becoming even more all-encompassing and efficient, the measures often lead to inconsistencies and irrationalities:

> why, for example, do we insist on the fulfilment of contribution conditions before granting a sickness benefit under National Insurance, whereas if the sickness can be shown to be due to an industrial accident or industrial disease contribution conditions do not have to be fulfilled in order to qualify for an even higher-rate of benefit (and of course there are no contribution conditions at all for the treatment of sickness under the National Health Service); ... why should the widow of an insured male who has died a natural death be treated quite differently from the widow of a man who has died as a result of an industrial accident; why should the widow who has no private means and so goes out to work in order to supplement her benefit be subjected to a means-test on her earnings and may have her benefit reduced, whereas the widow with substantial private means in the form of unearned income is not subject to the 'earnings rule'? [18]

We saw in our review of housing measures how subsidies were given and withdrawn in succession, depending on the government in power; hardly rational policy. As well as this:

> For years the Minister of Housing (or whatever his title may be) has set a target of the number of houses to be built annually, but one wonders how the actual figure is determined when within the

> Ministry there is no real knowledge of the actual stock of houses
> already built, their age, condition and estimated length of life, nor
> are systematic attempts made to measure the real future demands
> for new houses [19]

Indeed, the very division of the welfare state into separate government departments, both local and central, is illogical and inefficient. A family's housing, employment, schooling and financial problems will be dealt with by a large number of civil servants and local government employees with little or no co-ordination between them.

The second problem with a list of legislative measures is that it implies that statutory bodies are the only important participants. For Marxists the causes of poverty, ill health and unemployment lie in the socio-economic tensions within the capitalist system. Legislative measures can only be cosmetic in their effect, the problems will remain as long as the capitalist system does. To concentrate attention on legislation is to divert it from the really important issues; the search for profit, the consequent exploitation of the working class and the inherent economic contradictions which these produce. From another point of view R M Titmuss points out that:

> all collective interventions to meet certain needs of the individual
> and/or to serve the wider interests of society may now be broadly
> grouped into three major categories of welfare: social wefare, fiscal
> welfare and occupational welfare [20]

Social welfare includes the kinds of measures we have just examined, while fiscal welfare means benefits given through the tax system and occupational welfare those deriving from one's job. Fiscal benefits currently available include the tax allowance given to married men, allowances for dependents (for example the old, the incapacitated or infirm), allowances for mortgages and for life assurance policies (now abolished for *new* policies.) Occupational benefits include such things as occupational pensions, death benefits, subsidised meals, subscriptions to private medical schemes, cars, personal expenses for travel, entertainment, children's school fees and other benefits of enormous variety. The ultimate cost of these, says Titmuss 'falls in large measure on the Exchequer' as companies can claim tax relief for them. In addition to these benefits Titmuss and others stress that *statutory* measures are only part of the welfare state. Market Liberals in particular stress the importance of voluntary and religious bodies, charities, private insurance companies, public schools and even property developers within the welfare state. [21]

Theoretical Perspectives on Social Policy

In this section we will deal with four main perspectives: Social Democratic theory, Market Liberal theory, Marxism and Functionalism.[22] The first two approaches are based on the premise that complex social forms such as the welfare state are the product of the actions and decisions of individuals and that such institutions can be reformed or removed within a given social structure. The second two take the reverse stance, seeing the actions of the social structure as having a profound influence on its individual members and as constraining the range and forms of institutions that exist within it. These two opposing standpoints are often referred to as individualism and structuralism.

Social Democratic Theory

Graham Room in *The Sociology of Welfare*[23] includes within the Social Democratic school the following writers: R M Titmuss, T H Marshall, Peter Townsend, David Donnison and Brian Abel-Smith. As Room himself admits, there is a danger of distortion in 'lumping together' a group of different writers under one label, but he considers that they have sufficient in common for the attempt to be worthwhile.

One important characteristic shared by all members of this school is the view that the free-market system (unrestrained capitalism) involves a variety of undesirable features. These can be summarised as follows:[24]

1. Being based on greed, not social purpose, a free market economy leads to avoidable ills and misery for some.
2. Market forces are not controlled by the people, only a few big businessmen.
3. A free market system gives unjust rewards; rewards and failures are not governed by principle.
4. The market is not self-regulating and unless it is regulated from outside it will lead to economic crisis, unemployment, inflation and over-production.
5. As a result of the above factors poverty and inequality increase in a free market economy.

From the Social Democratic viewpoint the rise of the welfare state was due to the increasingly obvious drawbacks of the free-market:

> The welfare state was born in an era of moral shock and remorse caused by the revelation of the appalling conditions among the poor shown to exist by Charles Booth's great inquiry into the *Life and Labour of the People of London* and other investigations. A

sense of compassion combined with the pangs of conscience led to a middle and upper-class revolt against a state of affairs which had now become intolerable. A widespread feeling of shock and compassion for the helpless victims of circumstances beyond their control again erupted during the period of mass unemployment in the years between the two World Wars, and especially during the great depression[25]

A process of reform rather than radical change thus began; a process applauded by most Social Democrats. From their point of view it is necessary for the government to intervene in the market, compensating victims, redistributing income, providing opportunity for the underprivileged and restraining the greedy and powerful where necessary. The old, the poor, the sick, those with large families, the disabled and others are aided through the mediation of the state by the young, the affluent, the healthy and the single. Such intervention promotes social justice too, ensuring that those with ability are rewarded and that power and privilege are gained through merit, not birth. It helps make society more efficient by doing this, preventing wastage of ability and enabling all individuals to realise their full potential. In addition, social conflict is avoided and society integrated: all can support a manifestly fair system:

> the ways in which society organises and structures its social institutions—and particularly its health and welfare system—can encourage or discourage the altruistic in man; such systems can foster integration or alienation[26]

The aim of the Social Democrats is to promote a society where social priorities are set in a considered, rational way, with a co-ordinated plan to achieve them. In such a society social inequalities are reduced to acceptable levels, social ills are attacked by state controlled organisations such as the NHS, DHSS and social services departments. Private enterprise is either stimulated or checked by government as necessary. Social Democrats adopt the view that most people are likely to need help from the state in meeting crises and unforeseen circumstances during their lives. This is what has been termed the *institutional model* and is opposed to the *residual model* which sees those in need of help as a separate and quite small group. These different perspectives give rise to varying views on the need for and nature of state intervention. The table opposite sums up the differences between the two models.

P Townsend sums up the institutional model when he writes:

> The poor who are dependent on the social services are not a

Main Features	Residual	Institutional
State responsibility in meeting needs (ideology of state intervention)	minimal	optimal
Distribution of benefits based on means tests (selective) or available to all (universal)	selective	mainly universal
Range of state-provided services	limited	extensive
Population covered by state-provided services	few	most
Level of benefits and therefore level of state expenditure on them	low	medium
Use of means test	primary	secondary
Nature of clients	the poor	citizens
Status of clients	low	medium
Nature of service provided	coercive	helping
Role of non-statutory agencies in welfare (charities, voluntary organisations etc)	primary	secondary
Model of state intervention supported by	Market Liberals	Social Democrats
Definition of poverty	absolute	relative[27]

separate section of the population, like some tribe of untouchables living on the other side of a canyon ... A substantial part, and possibly a majority, of the population have known poverty at some time. Adversity is something which might strike universally and many people who are prosperous and healthy are glad of the security of the social services. Many of their nearest and dearest ... are dependent on these services. Security for oneself and one's family can strengthen morale and provide incentives at work. The web of social services is enmeshed with the daily life and thought of the nation ... The work of housewives and other 'dependents' releases men for industry and it would be improper to claim that they make no real contribution to production[28]

As the table indicates, most Social Democrats believe that state benefits should be *universal* ones, they should *not* be founded on a means test which assesses need but should be available to all, or at least all within a given section of the population. The retired, those with small children, the disabled, the unemployed and the sick[29] fall into this category. Arguments in support of universal benefits are as follows:

1. Universal benefits eliminate the need for a means test which is humiliating, involves bureaucratic form filling and interviews and smacks of charity, hence discouraging claimants from getting what is rightfully theirs. For the Social Democrat the problems of low take-up of means-tested benefit is an important failing of the current social security system. In 1977 there was a 77 per cent take-up for supplementary pensions, 74 per cent for supplementary benefit, 50 per cent for rent allowance and only 4 per cent for free welfare foods. No means-tested benefit had a take-up greater than 80 per cent.[30]

2. Universal benefits are funded from taxes and National Insurance contributions paid in the past by the people themselves. One should thus be able to withdraw benefits from the fund regardless of one's current financial circumstances. The Beveridge Report makes this point and elaborates on it, stating that there is a strong:

   popular objection to any kind of means test. This objection springs not so much from a desire to get everything for nothing, as from resentment at a provision which appears to penalise what people have come to regard as the duty and pleasure of thrift ... Payment of a substantial part of the cost of benefit as a contribution irrespective of the means of the contributor is the firm basis of a claim to benefit irrespective of means[31]

3. Universal benefits are far more practical, being cheaper to administer than selective ones. Administering the means tests costs a lot of money which should be spent on the benefits themselves. Moreover means tests cannot properly take account of the unique circumstances and needs that each individual or family has. They therefore represent an inaccurate form of selectivity.

4. Means tests help to maintain poverty because they create a 'poverty trap'. This means that when a person's earnings go up (for example by starting a part-time job after being unemployed for a time) they may become ineligible for some means-tested benefits (supplementary benefit in this instance) and hence their standard of living does not improve, indeed it may be reduced. Universal benefits are

paid regardless of other income and so prevent the poverty trap from operating.

5. Means tests can be used as a form of social control through the way the rules of eligibility are framed. People who live rough, who don't get married but only live together, who won't accept some types of jobs, who are in rent arrears and so on find that they may be deprived of some means-tested benefits.

6. Universal benefits are integrative, selective ones are divisive. When services are available to all there is no danger of a polarisation of society. P Townsend writes that a policy of introducing or extending means-tested benefits:

> misconceives the nature of poverty and reinforces the condition it is supposed to alleviate. The policy assumes that poverty is an absolute condition, a lack of minimum subsistence cash income, which requires little more than the diversion of a minute proportion of the national income in an efficient manner to alleviate it. It fosters hierarchical relationships of superiority and inferiority in society, diminishes rather than enhances the status of the poor and has the effect of widening rather than reducing social inequalities ... It distracts attention from the problems of improving the quality of public services and of expanding the resources available for the general welfare of the community. It also assumes that the circumstances of the poor can be greatly improved without changing major social institutions and severely limiting the opportunity of the prosperous sections of the community to accumulate more privileges[32]

Social Democrats are generally in favour of a reform of the welfare system. Suggestions often involve a unification of the tax and social security systems. The idea of simplification of the social security system has been around for some time, but a fully worked out scheme was recently proposed by the Basic Income Research Group, which consists of MPs, business people and academics. Under this scheme, everybody, regardless of income, would receive a basic payment from the state sufficient to enable them to live. Some, such as the chronically sick and disabled, would receive a larger amount. This would permit the abolition of the complex and administratively expensive system of benefits we have at the moment. Taxation would ensure that the better off 're-pay' the state for the benefit they too receive under this system. It would be a cheap scheme to administer, would abolish the distinction between claimants and non-claimants and hence the stigma attached to claiming benefits. It would ensure that all those in poverty received benefit by ending confusion over rights to benefit and thus non-claiming for whatever reason. The poverty trap would end, too, as benefit is received even when one also has a low-paid or part-time job. Other proposals involve a combined tax/benefit assessment form. The individual would fill it out each year and, depending on income and other factors, would either pay tax or receive 'negative tax', that is benefit.

Critics of these types of schemes agree that they are too expensive. Instead of introducing more universal benefits recent governments of both parties have moved towards means-tested ones. This is despite the fact that the stated aim of the legislation which immediately followed the Beveridge Report was to provide universal benefits and services where possible. Some universal benefits do remain. They include the National Health Service, State Education, National Insurance benefits and Child Benefit. Some benefits began as universal but were later made selective, usually because of cost. The most famous example is the withdrawal of free prescriptions, which were available for all until 1951[33].

This account of Social Democratic Theory has tended to over-generalise for the sake of clarity. Social Democrats are divided between themselves on how far reform without major institutional change can be effective, how far universalism alone is adequate without some element of selectivity and how extensive the range of state provided services should be. Moreover, Social Democratic Theory is not static. These writers change their positions during the development of their thought and as social and economic circumstances necessitate a review of their earlier positions.[34]

Market Liberal Theory

Included in this school are such writers as Adam Smith, J S Mill, Milton Friedman and F A Hayek. While Social Democrats see the faults in capitalism as arising from the unrestrained play of market forces, Market Liberals see them as the result of misguided attempts to restrain these forces. Market Liberals share the following assumptions about the role of the state in social policy:

1. State intervention coerces individuals and infringes their liberties. They do recognise that *some* state intervention is necessary so that an individual can pursue his/her own interests unmolested by others and to look after those who cannot look after themselves, such as the mentally ill. Any intervention beyond this minimum level though, is harmful.
2. State intervention above a minimum level is unnecessary. If the individual is permitted to pursue his or her interests acting either

alone or in *voluntary* association with others, he or she will also be acting in the common good. The individual capitalist not only creates profit for him/herself but also jobs and wages for the employees, goods for consumers and earnings for the country. If poverty or need exists then concerned individuals can be allowed to form voluntary associations which will operate much better than inflexible, bureaucratic organisations operating under statutory compulsion:

much for which the coercive action of the state is usually involved can be done better by voluntary collaboration[35]

3. State intervention to reduce inequality is misguided. Inequality provides incentive to improve one's position, stimulating hard work. The prospect of profit stimulates saving and investment which adds to the country's wealth. This would not be done if no advantage could be gained. Excessive inequality is avoided by the free play of market forces such as competition, supply and demand and free wage bargaining. For example in a free market, unemployment is avoided by a decline in wage levels, enabling capitalists to employ more people. Too much state power or the presence of monopolies of business or unions limits this free play and disrupts the system. If levels of poverty and need *should* fall below a certain minimum level in individual cases then the state and/or voluntary organisations should identify these cases and act to help them.

4. State intervention creates demand in groups for services and benefits to which they would have no right in the normal workings of the market system. Demands for free or cheap prescriptions place an intolerable burden on the whole economic system. The government monopoly over welfare services is inefficient and costly, being unregulated by price and profit mechanisms. Bureaucracy grows, planning is inflexible to need. The individual is increasingly at the mercy of institutions over which he/she has no real control.[36]

Clearly the Market Liberals adopt the residual model of social policy. The government, they believe, has too readily adopted the institutional approach and thus over-extended social services. What is required is a reduction in the scope of government intervention. This should include the introduction of means testing in all areas of services and benefits, a consequent reduction in the number of people served, a reduction in the level of financial benefits paid and a reduction in the number and type of services provided. Selective benefits are advocated by Market Liberals for the following reasons:

1. Means testing identifies those in true need and helps *them*. Selective benefits are thus truly redistributive in effect, if only to the very worst off. Universal benefits help the rich and the poor alike. They may actually be detrimental to the poor in some cases by encouraging the rich to compete with them for available resources. An example would be an increase in subsidies to the state education system. This would encourage rich parents of able children to leave the private education sector. The increased competition suffered by children from poorer backgrounds would probably more than outweight any benefits derived from the increased subsidy. Poor families require positive discrimination because they suffer from cultural as well as material deprivation, according to Market Liberals. Their 'culture of poverty' leads them to adopt fatalistic attitudes, to reject education, to be lazy and to demand immediate rather than deferred gratification. These are special obstacles which affect the very poor, the residual sector of society, and hence require special, not equal, treatment compared to other sectors.

2. Universal benefits mean that the resources of the welfare state have to be spread so thinly that they can never eliminate poverty, avoidable ill health or poor housing completely. Selective benefits are cheaper and therefore more effective in doing their job as the level of benefit can be high. In addition to this, the money saved by giving means tested benefits allows tax levels and National Insurance contributions to be lower. This increases the incentive to work harder, according to Market Liberals, and thus raises the general level of prosperity of the country.

3. Where services for all, free of charge, are provided the laws of supply and demand are upset and this disrupts the whole of the economy. For example, in housing, subsidies mean that council housing is more attractive than home ownership. This artificially lowers the prices that can be charged for private housing and this will result in bankruptcy for some building firms. This means higher levels of unemployment and the need for even more state spending.

Examples of means-tested benefits and services available today include: supplementary benefit, free school meals, free milk for young children, housing benefit and free home help services. The current Conservative government, adopting a Market Liberal perspective, has a policy of extending means testing where possible for these sorts of reasons. It is also in favour of extending the role of the private sector in the provision of welfare services. A Department of Health consultation paper was published in 1984 outlining proposals to switch the role of local authority social services departments to co-ordinators of services provided by private sector, voluntary and charitable agencies. Introducing these proposals, the Social Services Secretary said that social workers should consider 'value for money', and entrepreneurship as part of their work. Given an expenditure of £2.5 billion a year and a growing number of dependent people and those in need of help, social services departments could not be expected to cope alone. [37]

For Market Liberals such free-market economies as those of Hong Kong or the United States are the model which Britain ought to follow. M Friedman applauds the USA's approach to social policy:

> The welfare state has continued to progress; its citizens have become better fed, better clothed, better housed and better transported; ... All this has been the product of the initiative and drive of individuals co-operating through the free market ... The central defect of (government) measures is that ... they fail to resolve what is supposedly a conflict of interests ... not by establishing a framework that will eliminate the conflict ... but by forcing people to act against their own interests [38]

Britain needs to emulate the United States' free market policies in its attempt to eradicate the five giants. Squalor is eliminated by selling council houses and abolishing rent control. The very poor should be helped to find accommodation by giving them benefits so they can afford the market rent. Ignorance is best tackled by the introduction of a selection process to identify those who will benefit most from high-standard education. The introduction of loans rather than grants for students will ensure incentive to succeed, and the expansion of private schooling supplemented by state help for poor families with bright children. Want is eliminated by government help for the very poor to bring them up to the subsistence level. Any greater degree of assistance would destroy incentives to work. High levels of National Insurance contributions or taxes also destroy incentive and put private insurance companies out of business, further disrupting the market. Disease should be dealt with by private insurance schemes and private medical companies. Free state medical services eliminate choice for the patient and are too much of an economic burden on the state. In the NHS, the aged and the mentally ill deprive of treatment those who could contribute to the economy but are temporarily ill. They represent a double burden on the economy. [39] Idleness (unemployment) is not a necessary consequence of capitalism for the Market Liberal. Its abolition is achieved by limiting the power of trade unions and reducing social security benefits which together allow wages to fall to their 'correct' level. This is the point at which capitalists find it cheaper to employ workers than to replace them with an auto-mated process. Lower wage levels also improve a nation's international trading position. This stimulates its economy.

To sum up, Market Liberals see advanced industrial societies as meritocracies. These are systems which allow social position to be achieved through the application of ability to tasks. State intervention beyond a minimum level in the operation of society and the economy disrupts the workings of this meritocracy and can only have detrimental effects.

Marxist Theory

Included within this school are such writers as C Offe, J Saville, R Miliband, H Westergaard, J Resler, N Poulantzas, N Ginsberg and J O'Connor. All share the view that the capitalist system is founded upon exploitation and conflict of interest. All believe that the welfare state cannot eradicate the five giants while it continues to operate in the context of a capitalist system. They are divided on the reasons for the existence of an apparently humanitarian system of welfare within an exploitative society. There are three types of argument which Marxists present to explain this:

1. The view that the welfare state is a concession which the working class has won from capitalists through trade unions, political action and direct action such as demonstrations and riots. Marx himself takes this standpoint, seeing the early Factory Acts as the product of the workers' concerted action against oppression and exploitation:

   for Marx, the mainspring of progress was working class action and factory legislation was 'the victory of a principle', of the 'political economy of the working class' over the 'political economy of the middle class'. In short, Marx recognises that workers need not wait 'with folded arms' for the day of revolution but could begin to establish socialist values and institutions, piecemeal, within the bourgeois society. This, for Marx, was the main significance of social legislation such as the factory act[40]

The ability of the working class to extract concessions from the bourgeoisie depends upon the degree to which each class is unified and therefore strong. It also depends on the nature of the demands made by the working class; whether they fundamentally threaten the way the system is organised or are more limited in nature. Finally it depends on the state of the economy at the time the demands are made; in a time of crisis the capitalist class cannot make concessions which would cut dangerously into profitability.

2. The view that the welfare state is a 'safety valve', constructed by the capitalist class to avoid political and economic disturbance to the system. The capitalists make minor concessions on limited areas of policy to prevent fundamental redistribution through radical movements. H Westergaard writes that:

> conflict is regulated through a series of compromises which define, not only the means and procedures of conflict, but also the area of conflict ... only a small band of the full range of alternative policies is effectively ventilated and disputed[41]

The idea of giving concessions to avoid future trouble has been made explicit by statesmen quite regularly. Sir Ian Gilmour, a prominent Conservative and a critic of Mrs Thatcher, insisted in a speech at the Cambridge Union in 1980 that the state would not survive if people did not feel loyalty to it. The way to win that loyalty was to ensure that they gain from state protection. He asked, 'If the state is not interested in them why should they be interested in the state?'[42] Conservatives like Gilmour were the dominant forces in the Party during the 50's, 60's and early 70's. Now they are in the minority. Gilmour's speech represented an attack on what he saw as the dangerous cuts in benefits being made by the Conservative government at the time.

3. The view that the welfare state operates in the interests of the capitalists, representing minimal cost but considerable gain to them. Some Marxists argue that *every* aspect of the welfare state operates in the capitalists' interests. We will follow N Ginsberg's analysis of the way the social security system does this.

Ginsberg argues that the social security benefits scheme:

> attempts to reproduce the immediate capital-labour relation in a number of ways. Above all it is concerned with the reproduction and maintenance of the reserve army of labour[43]

The presence of a group of 'stand-by workers' on low levels of benefit acts as a threat to those in work. It makes them quiescent, willing to work for low wages and willing to accept jobs of low status, skill and pay because the alternative (being replaced by one of the unemployed and finding oneself in the dole queue) is even more unpleasant. Furthermore, those on the dole have an obligation to seek full time work. If there *is* an upturn in the economy they can rapidly be put to work to increase production. By limiting eligibility to claim benefit, the social security system ensures that the *family* has to bear the financial burden in the case of such groups as married women and students who themselves represent a reserve of cheap and unprotected labour power. This reinforces women's dependence on men and implicitly supports the notion that 'woman's place is in the home'.[44] Lastly, the social security system imposes discipline and restraint on the working class by denying benefit to those who go on strike or resign (benefit can be withheld for six weeks in the latter circumstance.) Those who fight against, or reject the exploitative nature of capitalism find themselves unsupported by its welfare system. In addition the principle that workers should contribute not only through taxation but also National Insurance payments keeps an army of over 10,000 clerks employed in the DHSS office in Newcastle. Their job is to keep track of the contribution and benefit record of every insured person, despite the fact that income from National Insurance contributions pays for only a fraction of the social security system. This provides jobs for the middle class instead of real benefits for the poor. The distinction between contributory benefits (unemployment benefit or pensions) and non-contributory benefits (like supplementary benefit) helps to maintain the distinction between the 'deserving' and the 'undeserving' poor and to give the contributing worker a stake in the state. Thus what appears to be a 'gift' from the state to the worker is in fact a further tool in the oppression of the worker according to Ginsberg. He does recognise, though, that working class pressure through spontaneous direct action, the party system and the trade unions serves to moderate the exploitative nature of the welfare system.

In addition to the reinforcement of the structure of capitalism, the provision of a welfare state makes it work more efficiently. Healthy, well-housed and reasonably well educated workers are more efficient than those who live in disease, squalor and ignorance. Furthermore, as we shall see (page 148-149) some Marxists argue that the costs of the welfare state do not involve redistribution from the rich to the poor, but can be met mainly by payments from the more affluent sections of the working class.

These three approaches to the welfare state within capitalism are not mutually contradictory. J Saville, for example, sees the development of the welfare state as the result of the interaction of all three factors.[45] Most adhere to the view that the welfare state is a response to the functional necessities of capitalism.

Some Marxists believe that conditions for the working class can be marginally improved and inequalities reduced by changes and reforms in the operation of the welfare state. V George and P Wilding comment:

> the Marxist view of the individual social services is very similar to the Fabian (Social Democratic) view. In education, the main demands are comprehensive schools, nursery education, expansion

of higher education, reduction in the size of classes, more and better paid teachers and the abolition of private schools. In housing, there have been suggestions for the nationalisation of urban land for house building purposes, low interest rates to local authorities and owner-occupiers, restriction of private landlordism and greater legal security for all tenants against eviction and harassment ... The NHS is generally treated as a better specimen of socialist welfare provision than the other social services. Apart from improvements in buildings and manpower and the abolition of all charges and of private practice within the NHS, there is little fundamental criticism of the service[46]

However, the welfare state alone cannot abolish poverty, the ill health which results from unhealthy products and poor environmental and work conditions, nor inequalities in housing and education. These are rooted in the class structure itself. Ralf Miliband writes:

the truth—and it is a bitter truth—is that the abolition of poverty will have to wait until the abolition of the system which breeds it comes onto the agenda and this is a question which far transcends the issue of poverty itself[47]

Thus George and Wilding's statement may refer to a mild version of the Marxist case. Such reformist policies cannot hope to change or modify the class structure, though they may help the individual. In doing so it is possible that they are counter-productive for the working class. By making conditions marginally more comfortable within capitalism they postpone the day of revolution.

Functionalist Theory

Members of the functionalist school include E Durkheim, T Parsons, R Merton and N J Smelser. The basic elements of functionalist theory have been set out in the chapter on the Sociology of Knowledge (see pages 13-21). Here we are concerned with how this theory relates to social policy and administration. The three most important features of the theory in this respect are:

1. The view of society as a set of inter-related institutions.
2. The analysis of these social institutions in terms of the function they fulfil.
3. The whole structure is seen as being more powerful than any of its individual parts and thus operating a determining influence upon them.

Most functionalists see societies as moving through a course of development from a *simple* form, through an *intermediate* one to the *modern* form. During this transition the number of institutions in society becomes greater and the functions they perform more specialised. Thus in simple societies welfare functions, like many others, were provided by the extended kinship network. In intermediate types of society they were performed by religious institutions, along with the other functions those institutions fulfilled. In modern society welfare functions are performed by a range of specialised institutions: the NHS, the education system and social services departments. In any society of the modern type it is necessary for these forms of institutions to exist in order that the functions they fulfil be properly performed. Such institutions perform an integrative function, which we will now examine.

Welfare and Social Integration

As we saw earlier (page 16) integration is one of the four functional prerequisites of any society according to T Parsons. An integrative function is one that reduces conflict within the system and enhances feelings of solidarity and order. As the institutions in society become more numerous and more specialised (and therefore more diverse) there is a danger of breakdown in social integration. The division of labour can easily lead to anomie, a feeling of dependency on others and the feeling of failure or the fear of it. R Titmuss, writing with an acknowledged debt to Durkheim, says this:

> the dominating operative factor has been the increasing division of labour in society and, simultaneously, a great increase in labour specificity. This is perhaps one of the outstanding social characteristics of the twentieth century; the fact that more and more people consciously experience at one or more stages in their lives the process of selection and rejection; for education, for work, for vocational training, for professional status, for promotion, for opportunities of access to pension schemes, for collective social benefits ... (etc). In some senses at least, the arbiters of opportunity and of dependency have become, in their effects, more directly personal, more culturally demanding, more psychologically threatening ... as man becomes more individual and more specialised he becomes more socially dependent. This is of primary importance in understanding the development of systems of welfare; this and the fact that, simultaneously, man becomes more aware of what has caused his dependency, and thus

more exposed to uncertainty and conflict about the purposes and roles he himself is expected to fulfil[48]

In view of this threat to the established order it becomes necessary to set up a uniting welfare state; one which keeps a highly divided society together. Titmuss writes that:

> All collectively provided services are designed to meet certain socially recognised 'needs'; they are manifestations, first, of society's will to survive as an organic whole and, secondly, of the expressed wish of all the people to assist the survival of some people. Thus the post war welfare developments in Britain were connected with the demand for one society; for non-discriminatory services for all without distinction of class, income or race; for services ... which would deepen and enlarge self-respect; for services which would meaningfully encourage social integration[49]

Titmuss himself is not convinced that the social service agencies are doing a good job in fulfilling this integrative function in Britain. He says that they are, if anything 'enlarging and consolidating the area of social inequality.' Parsons and Smelser take a more positive view of the successes of modern welfare insitutions, even though they come from America, where state welfare is limited. Smelser writes, for example:

> whereas ... integrative exigencies (necessities) were faced by kinsmen, neighbours, and local largesse (charity) in pre-modern settings, development gives birth to dozens of institutions and organisations geared to these new integrative problems—labour recruitment agencies and exchanges, labour unions, government regulation of labour allocation, welfare and relief arrangements, co-operation societies, and savings institutions[50]

Closely linked to the idea of welfare measures as ensuring social integration is T H Marshall's discussion of citizenship rights. Though not a functionalist theorist himself (we have included him amongst the Social Democrats) his ideas have been adopted by such functionalists as T Parsons. Marshall argues that citizenship rights in Britain (and we can surmise, in other advanced industrial societies) involve three elements:[51]

1. *Civil rights.* These are the right of individual liberty and the rule of law without distinction of status, colour or age. In Britain they developed during the eighteenth century. The legal institutions of a country ensure that these rights are not contravened.
2. *Political rights.* These include the right to vote for all over a certain age, and the right of all to seek political office without regard to

wealth or social position. These rights are set out by statute and slowly evolved over a period of centuries, but developed particularly in the nineteenth century in Britain.
3. *Social rights*. These include the right to enjoy at least a minimum level of income so that one can share in the normal life of society and be accepted by its members. These rights are ensured by the operation of the welfare state. As we have seen, social rights have been most fully developed in the twentieth century, and particularly since the Second World War.

As societies move from the agrarian to the industrial form they first bestow civil rights (initially only in a limited way.)Political rights follow (which are gradually extended to cover lower sections of the stratification system and both sexes) and finally social rights (at first only for the absolutely destitute, later to the whole population thanks to universal provision) according to Marshall. The relationship between the three is an interdependent one. The development of the first aids ·that of the second and this the third, which in turn reinforces the others. Social rights provide the material comfort and a sense of community which allows civil and political rights to operate. Social rights therefore serve to *integrate* society, ensuring that there are no great inequalities in status or in opportunities to exercise civil or political rights. This is despite the fact that laissez-faire capitalism has an inherent tendency to produce inequalities of income, wealth and power. Marshall suggests the aim of welfare measures is not to reduce these inequalities, but to ensure that the social system remains stable despite their presence by providing social rights for all. In this sense they are functional, but are not egalitarian. In Marshall's view, any redistribution of income is within the working class rather than from the top to the bottom of the social stratification system. His account of the development of the three forms of rights lacks any account of conflict, of a fight by deprived groups to wrest concessions from advantaged groups. His description of the gentle evolution of rights without discord is very functionalist in tone. As our discussion of legislation to eliminate want has shown, the process was full or reversals and static periods. From a conflict perspective these are the result of the waxing powers and fortunes of working class movements in pressing for social rights.

Implicit in all this is the determinist notion that society *must* develop certain types of social institutions if it is to survive. Functionalists see *all* modern societies as *converging* towards an identical state regardless of any socio-economic differences between them in the past. The functional requirements of the economic system *necessitate* certain welfare arrangements, and the more advanced a society becomes, the more pressing this necessity. The details of the convergence theory are set out in Clark Kerr's *Industrialism and Industrial man*[52] and are neatly summarised by R Mishra as follows:

> Industrialisation transforms the nature of the labour force: the 'self-employed'—the farmers, craftsmen and the like—are replaced by workers 'employed' for a wage. Regular income from employment comes to be the main source of livelihood for an increasing proportion of the work force. Industrial employment also imposes a clear-cut distinction between those at work and those out of work. As a result, unemployment, sickness, work injury, old age and the like can bring about a sudden interruption in earnings, and the problem of protection against such contingencies becomes acute. Through urbanisation, industrial development also gives rise to problems of public health, housing and control of the urban environment. Industrial society also requires an educated work force and citizenry. Educating the masses thus becomes a key imperative. Alongside these changes, geographical and occupational mobility increases and the traditional agencies of support—the extended family and the local community—weaken. Thus the stage is set for the development of a host of formally organised patterns—friendly society benefits, charitable assistance, enterprise and state programmes, for example—to meet a variety of emergent needs. In short, industrialisation creates the preconditions for a substantial growth of specialised or 'structurally differentiated' agencies of welfare

The form of society and welfare system which results is:

> characterised as that of 'pluralistic industrialism'. Essentially, this is a 'mixed' system—one that lies somewhere between the extremes of total state control ('monism') and unremitting laissez-faire ('atomism'). In the case of welfare this means a position akin to the 'institutional' pattern. It is primarily the two extremes, the middle class and the communist societies that move towards the middle ground. In the former, laissez-faire and market-based distribution is gradually superseded by a measure of state responsibility and provision for basic needs while in the latter, total state control over resources and their distribution gives way to a more pluralistic arrangement[53]

A mixed system, including both state control and elements of laissez-faire is necessary because the high division of labour requires co-ordination through central control, but a certain degree of autonomy for component parts to ensure greatest efficiency and initiative is also required.

Like Marxists, functionalists see the demands of the system as determining, in large measure, the nature of the welfare institutions within it. Both adopt a structuralist rather than individualist perspective. In this as in other areas, though, functionalists stress consensus, integration and harmony while Marxists stress discord, conflict and exploitation.

Criticisms of the Four Perspectives on the Welfare State

The Social Democratic Approach

Because it takes an empirical rather than a theoretical approach it tends to concentrate on manifest characteristics of social problems rather than their causes; on symptoms rather than the disease. It was, for example, members of the Social Democratic school such as Brian Abel Smith and Peter Townsend who re-discovered poverty in such studies as *The Poor and the Poorest,* published in 1965. Peter Townsend in *Poverty in the UK* has attempted to identify those in poverty in more specific terms to help in the fight to eliminate it. From a Marxist point of view, though:

> This definition of problems and objectives carries certain risks. The risks are those in the first instance of identifying, or seeming to identify, poverty as a distinct condition to be studied, and perhaps remedied, without reference to the larger organisation of economy and society. It is true that much research on poverty today starts from premises which repudiate such an approach. Poverty is defined in relative, not in absolute terms, by reference to a more or less regularly rising average standard of living; and it arises, by that definition, from the general distribution of resources in society. Yet although this is a common starting point, its implications can fairly readily be forgotten. For to focus on poverty requires one to draw an arbitrary dividing line—sometimes, more reasonably, several alternative lines—to distinguish the 'poor' from the rest. Whatever precautionary statements accompany this, the effect can easily be to emphasize the specific to the neglect of the general. Poverty by contemporary definition in Britain, for example, is concentrated among the old, the sick, the disabled, large families, 'fatherless' families, and families dependent on earners in low-income jobs. But if attention is

focused on these categories, it takes more than just occasional statement of the point to remember that their conditions are extreme manifestations of the wider class-structured pattern of inequality in economy and society at large. All workers—manual and increasingly the routine non-manual—are vulnerable: liable to the hazards of poverty or near-poverty in old age, in sickness, on a change of family circumstances, on redundancy or short-time, in the later years of working life. Their vulnerability even in 'affluence' is quite different from the security which characterises middle- and upper-class life cycles, and which derives, not only from higher incomes, but from career patterns with cumulative increments, promotion prospects and fringe benefits; from possession or likelihood of inheritance of poverty, even on a limited scale; from material and other aid often available at critical points from relatives; from easier access to, and affinity in com-munication with, the supporting institutions of everyday life—educational, legal, social, administrative and health services[54]

There is an implicit conservatism in this approach; the fundamental nature of capitalism which gives rise to poverty is obscured in the detailed attention given to specific examples of poverty. Social Demo-crats can't see the wood from the trees.

N Ginsberg, the Marxist writer, suggests that the Social Democrats as the:

exponents of social administration have, in a sense, acted as the organic intellectuals for the liberal bourgeoisie, guiding the welfare state and developing its ideology and practice to meet new problems[55]

With their stress on gradual reform and improvement of the present system, without changing its fundamental nature, they miss the *real* reason for poverty, educational failure and so on: the inequality and exploitation on which capitalist society is based. Even Peter Townsend, whose approach comes closest to that of the Marxists, falls into this trap. He sees poverty as resulting from the hierarchical and highly unequal nature of our society, in terms of both financial means and power. Yet he too believes that the abolition of excessive wealth and income, the abolition of unemployment and breaking down the distinction between earners and dependents is possible within the confines of capitalism and could lead to the abolition of poverty. For a Marxist like J C Kincaid, the author of *Poverty and Equality in Britain,* such a view is naive. Kincaid believes that poverty cannot be abolished within capitalism. A new form of society, a socialist one, must first be created. Here social policy would be determined by human needs, not the profit motive. The needs of the poor and the old would have priority over the need for investment and profit. Concern for the health of workers would come before the profitability of the product or the demand for efficiency. Good standard housing for all would be provided before expensive luxury accommodation for the few. To merely *ask* the rich and powerful to give up their privilege in the name of philanthropy will never bring about these changes.

A related point is that, without an explicit theory, Social Democrats concentrate on the social problems which are widely accepted as such (for example poverty) and ignore others which explicit theory might point to (for example the inherent contradictions in capitalism which lead to overproduction and underconsumption.)

The functionalist might argue that while Social Democrats generally stress individualism and voluntarism, they are often forced into recognising the constraints that the structure puts upon the exercise of free will. Thus Titmuss in *The Gift Relationship* suggests that individuals should be allowed more freedom of choice for the expression of altruism. Nevertheless he writes about the necessity of a structured state welfare system in order to fulfill the integrative function, as we saw earlier. There is, in other words, an uncomfortable relationship between explicit individualism and implicit structuralism in much Social Democratic thought.

The Market Liberal Approach

Firstly, Social Democrats and Marxists both stress, to varying extents, the fact that unrestrained laissez-faire capitalism has harmful effects on some in society. It does not operate in the interests of all as Market Liberals claim. Marx himself points out that the search for profitability and efficiency in a competitive environment forces capitalists to introduce technology, which must eventually lead to large scale unemployment. Social Democrats stress that those too weak or ill or old to work tend to be forgotten in a system which emphasises rewards for productive effort. Both perspectives recognise that periods of crisis in the world economic system can lead to hardship for many. The view that leaving things alone is a policy which will benefit all in the long run is a mistaken one.

The individualism of Market Liberals can be criticised from a structuralist standpoint. Functionalists would argue that the unrestrained pursuit of self interest is not an adequate basis for social functioning. E Durkheim, for example, argues that agreed contracts between individuals must be founded upon common values about the meaning and operation of the contract and the society in which it is drawn up. P Taylor-Gooby and J Dale put this point succinctly:

> in most social settings the power of, for example, the police (and, more so, the environmental health officer) is to do with shared values, in this case, respect for civil authority and the idea that law and order represent a common interest ... It seems that the legitimacy of a particular form of society rests (at least) on the fact that considerable numbers of its members have similar favourable beliefs about it, and that this shared opinion contributes to the formation of institutions which socialize the young, incorporate or control deviants and generally contribute to the continuance of the social order[56]

For the functionalist, then, it is necessary to have state intervention in society not only to co-ordinate a highly complex division of labour, but to strengthen collective sentiments and integrate the people by supporting the common value system. The Market Liberals' conception of society as an aggregation of independent individuals is therefore misfounded.

Marxists see Market Liberal theory as ideological. We noted earlier (page 3) that Marx sees forms of knowledge as resulting from the interests of groups in particular social locations. Market Liberal theory is one which supports, albeit unconsciously, the interests of the capitalist class. Marx criticises Adam Smith, an early Market Liberal, for portraying the way people behave in capitalism as merely being part of human nature, the instinctive and natural way to behave. Instead it is an alienated, one-sided, degraded form of human interaction, far from what would be normal in a classless, non-exploitative society:

> According to Adam Smith, *society* is a *commercial enterprise.* Every one of its members is a *salesman.* It is evident how political economy establishes an *alienated* form of social intercourse as the *true and original* form, and that which corresponds to human nature[57].

R M Titmuss criticises many of the assumptions made by Market Liberals as being factually inaccurate. These include:

1. That Beveridge's aims have been achieved. They have not.
2. That there has been a transfer of resources from the rich to the poor. There has not.
3. That it is possible to identify who has paid for and who has benefited

from the welfare state. It is not, partly because of the very broad nature of social services (including within that term fiscal benefits, occupational benefits, as Titmuss does.)

4. That ... 'it is practicable, desirable and has any meaning in a complex society undergoing rapid and widespread change to abstract a "social service world" from the greater society, and to consider the functions and effects of the part without reference to the life of the whole'.[58] In other words the Market Liberals' residual model of welfare is a misguided one.

The Marxist Approach

The most common criticism of the Marxist approach to social policy is that while it attacks the structure of welfare services in capitalism, it provides no workable alternative. Marxists are strangely silent about answers to questions concerning communism. Who is to decide which groups are in need? Who decides how much they will get? If the state has disappeared (as Marx said it would) how is the practical administration of welfare to be achieved? Marxism is very negative, dismissing present arrangements without making proposals for improvement but merely pointing to a vague future society.

Social Democrats criticise Marxists for not appreciating the important effects of individual and collective efforts to ameliorate conditions within capitalism. They criticise the deterministic nature of Marxists' structuralism and suggest instead that society can be shaped and improved within a given economic structure. Welfare arrangements are seen, in this view, as relatively independent of determination by class interests.

An important area of criticism is that Marxists have tended to adopt a functionalist explanation of the welfare services. They consider, as Ginsberg does, that such services help to maintain the social system. This lays Marxists open to the same sort of criticism often levelled at functionalists:

1. that their explanations are *tautological,* they explain the *origins* of social institutions in terms of their consequences. A logically circular argument and hence invalid.
2. They isolate only a *limited* range of the consequences of social measures, ignoring others. For example, Ginsberg stresses the effects of the social security system in terms of work incentives. He ignores its beneficial effects for the unemployed and other groups who claim benefit through it.

3. Structurally orientated Marxist writers at least ignore the importance of conflict within the system for extracting concessions from the dominant class and thus establishing systems of welfare which are *not* functional for the bourgeoisie. Marx cannot be accused of this, but many later Marxists can.

Mishra points out in criticism of Marxists that they tend to focus on capitalist societies alone and ignore the evidence of welfare systems operating in such socialist societies as the USSR. This means that Marxist analysis fails to distinguish adequately between capitalism and industrialism as related but analytically separable influences on the development of welfare. Secondly, Marxism fails to realise that some of the problems of welfare in capitalism may result not from the inherent contradictions of capitalism itself but from its democratic nature in the West. Thirdly, Marxists would appreciate the practical problems of welfare in a socialist society if they studied attempts to set up welfare systems in such societies. However, recent Marxism has tended to be very theoretical, indeed anti-empirical, in approach and so these kinds of studies have not been done.

The Functionalist Approach

Like much recent Marxist writing, functionalist work is so theoretical and general in nature that it is not very helpful in terms of practical policy proposals.

Marxists criticise functionalism for ignoring conflict and division within society, and for their exaggerated stress on consensus, shared goals and common interests. This leads functionalist writers to ignore the fact that welfare arrangements may be functional for some groups but not for others. For example the contributory principle in social security is useful for clerical workers (it provides them with employment) and for employers and governments (who can recover the cost of *their* contribution to the National Insurance fund from workers through increased prices and taxes respectively) but not for workers themselves. For them it represents an additional tax on earnings and may result in incligibility for certain kinds of benefit due to non-fulfilment of contribution conditions. It is more useful to think in terms of the *consequences,* both intended and unintended, of policy rather than its functions. If one is only looking for functional consequences of policy one only tends to find functional consequences; the others are ignored.

Individualists and voluntarists are critical of the functionalists' structuralism and determinism. Like Marxists, functionalists ignore the

127

power of individual actors and of groups (for example political parties) to change or reform the existing social welfare system. Functionalists place too much emphasis on the needs of the whole system which result in certain institutional forms within it. International comparisons demonstrate that societies which are very similar economically have very different patterns of welfare and, furthermore, do not appear to be converging towards a middle ground. The USA and the UK have very different educational systems and quite different levels of provision of state funded health care. There are vast differences in provision of social security in advanced industrial societies, ranging from none for the uninsured to the British supplementary benefit system. There are enormous differences in the provision of council housing, ranging from none to about 30 per cent of the total stock. Such comparisons undermine the functionalist theory of convergence, as does an examination of policies relating to the welfare state *within* one country. Far from there being a trend in one direction, driven by the functional necessities of industrialism, policy is apt to undergo changes of direction, even U-turns. Conservative Party policy has moved away from the basic agreement with the Labour Party about the need for the state to accept responsibility for basic provision (part of what has been called Butskellism—policies associated both with the Conservative R A Butler and Labour's H Gaitskell.) It now advocates firm treatment for 'malingerers' and strikers, charges for certain services, private health and welfare schemes and more voluntary welfare services. This new approach to social services and benefits makes one question the validity of the theory of undirectional convergence and of the gradual development of citizenship rights. Far from becoming more prevalent, Marshall's social rights appear to be losing ground at the moment.

Many critics of functionalism, particularly Marxists, have noted how it implicitly supports the status quo. R Mishra writes:

> with a consensus view of society functionalism can scarcely avoid identifying with the ruling powers. Thus seemingly neutral concepts like 'integration' and 'social control' serve to conceal the question of power, of class relations and inequality involved in different forms of social policy

Furthermore its 'value-free' approach means that:

> its major concepts do not help in the critical evaluation of social institutions. And this limits the uses of functionalism from the standpoint of the evaluation and formulation of social policy[59]

The Effects of Social Policy

In this section we examine the impact that social policy has had on each of the five giants. This is done by looking at the evidence on the existence of poverty, disease, ignorance, squalor and unemployment in Britain today. Where relevant, we also look at the information on inequalities in these five areas across the social stratification systems. We avoid trying to answer the question 'has the welfare state achieved its aims?' because those aims are subject to numerous interpretations. They could simply involve the 'killing' of the five giants. They are more likely to involve a number of other objectives: social control, social integration, social stability and economic efficiency. Each of the perspectives has something different to say on this, and even in government circles it is clear that the stated aims of policy are not the whole story. Much is left unstated, at least in public, and often the effects of policy are not those which were initially desired. For these reasons, we confine our attention to the actual effects of social welfare policy measures.

Want

Before we can examine the extent of poverty on modern Britain we must first make it clear exactly what is meant by that term. V George and P Wilding, after a critical analysis of the literature, identify six different definitions:[60]

1. A subjective definition; that perceived by the majority of the population as being the minimum amount required to make ends meet:

    > public opinion studies tend to see poverty in subsistence terms but, even so, in more generous terms than what is possible under the government's minimum standard

    It is, in fact, about 75 per cent higher than the levels of supplementary benefit.
2. A definition in terms of income levels in the country; usually the lowest tenth on the income distribution scale. This is a relative definition as it defines the poor in terms of the income of the rest.
3. The absolute definition of poverty is the objectively determined minimum of income below which it is impossible to remain fit and healthy. This is the subsistence level. It is adopted by many Market Liberals.
4. The official definition of poverty is the level of payments under the supplementary benefit scheme. There are long term rates and short

term rates, the former 27 per cent higher than the latter. Many claimants receive additional payments to the basic supplementary benefit rates. In addition some groups (the elderly and widows) receive more generous treatment than others (the homeless and unmarried mothers.) This is not a fixed poverty line at all. This is especially so, as even the value of basic payments fluctuate over time with the effects of inflation and periodic increases by the Chancellor.

5. A relative definition which takes into account the cost of items considered necessary in the type of society one is considering.

6. A relative definition which takes into account not only the cost of *items* considered essential in a particular society but also the cost of maintaining a normal life-style. This is one of the definitions used in P Townsend's *Poverty in the United Kingdom.*[61]

Other Social Democrats find it too extreme a definition: to eliminate it would mean everybody living a similar lifestyle, all having a cooked breakfast, holidays, similar housing conditions and educational opportunities. They also point to the fact that one's lifestyle is as much to do with personal preference as income. Just because I do not eat a roast lunch on Sunday does not mean I am poor.[62] Marxists point out that it gives the misleading impression that *absolute* poverty has been abolished in Britain, which it has not. However Townsend says that he can identify a threshold of income below which people's ability to live a normal life is seriously impaired. This is about 50 per cent above the basic level of supplementary benefit.

How far has poverty been eliminated in Britain today? The easiest definition to take to answer this question is **4**.

All national estimates, with the exception of Townsend's *Poverty in the United Kingdom* are based on the government's family expenditure surveys which take supplementary benefit levels as their yardstick. The table outlines the relative position over a period of twenty-one years. We must remember that benefit scales have risen substantially over the years so figure are not directly comparable.

Number of Individuals with Incomes below the Supplementary Benefit Level, Great Britain

Year	Individuals Number (Millions)	%
1960	1.990	3.8
1972	1.780	3.4
1977	2.020	4.0
1981	2.810	5.3 [63]

Townsend's research, based on interviews of 10,000 people in 1968-1969 throughout the United Kingdom (with in-depth surveys in Salford, Glasgow, Belfast and Neath) suggests that there were 3.48 million people (6.4%) below the supplementary benefit level (Townsend 1979 p 275 Table 7.2.) This suggests that the government estimates are optimistic.

How does the supplementary benefit poverty line compare with the others? The first definition is 75 per cent above it, as we saw earlier. In terms of a percentage of average earnings (definition 2) the short-term rates of benefit for a single householder represented 25.6 per cent of the average male workers' salary in 1979. For a married couple they represented 39.4 per cent of that salary. In both cases this was an improvement on the value of benefits in 1948 (which were then 22.9 per cent and 36.1 per cent respectively.) The long term rates were 33.1 per cent and 50.0 per cent for a single householder and married couple respectively, these percentages having remained roughly the same since 1966. [64]

Whether supplementary benefit rates represent an absolute poverty line is difficult to say. After reviewing evidence which demonstrates that supplementary benefit levels are not sufficient to allow claimants to buy clothing and other goods above a rigorous minimum level, George and Wilding state:

> supplementary benefit rates were inadequate in 1948 and, in spite of some improvement over the years, they remain inadequate today. How inadequate the scales are is impossible to say without a thorough study by the government to identify and cost those needs that must be adequately covered by the supplementary benefit rates today [65]

It seems that if supplementary benefit levels are above the absolute poverty line, they are not far above it. They certainly do not even approximate to the levels of poverty suggested in definitions 5. and 6. Townsend found that adopting a type 5. definition, there were 5 million people (9.2 per cent of the population) in poverty in 1968. These were people with an income of less than 50 per cent of the mean household income.

Taking his type 6. definition, which attempts to assess life-style deprivation, Townsend found 12.46 million people (22.9 per cent of the population) in poverty. [66]

How is it possible for so many people (2.8 million in 1981 at a conservative estimate) to fall below the state's safety net, the non-contributory supplementary benefit level? George and Wilding suggest that there are three main reasons:

1. Many people do not claim this means-tested benefit. About one million in 1978 according to the Supplementary Benefits Commission.
2. People in full time employment cannot claim supplementary benefit. Although they could claim family income supplement (see page 88), many do not; and anyway this can be below the supplementary benefit level in many cases.
3. People who lose their jobs through misconduct, who resign, who 'unreasonably' refuse jobs or training may be refused supplementary benefit for up to six weeks and then only receive a reduced amount. Workers on strike are not entitled to claim the full amount of supplementary benefit.

Thus Beveridge's stated aim to provide a minimum level of income for all has not been achieved. The old, the unemployed, single parent families, large families, the disabled, the long-term sick, and those on low pay are the groups most likely to find themselves in poverty, according to P Townsend.

On the positive side, The Royal Commission on the Distribution of Income and Wealth, reporting in 1978, showed that 22.7 per cent of individuals would have been below the supplementary benefit level had it not been for social security benefits. After payments this figure was reduced to only 3.3 per cent according to their estimates.[67] Thus the social security system has been 85 per cent successful in raising people to a minimum level of income. Expenditure on social security increased from 5.5 per cent of GNP in 1951 to 10.4 per cent in 1980. However, the rising level of expenditure may simply reflect the growing numbers of people thrown into circumstances in which they require the help of the state. It is unfortunately the case that the administrative problems which existed in previous years still remain, despite the increase in expenditure:

> dingy offices, long queues, harassed and low-paid clerical officers; erratic treatment of different claimants; low rate of take-up due to ignorance, lack of organisation, administrative evasiveness, malpractice, inefficiency and pride. The needs of significant groups are not adequately met, especially those of one-parent families and the long-term unemployed[68]

Disease
Disease cannot be eliminated completely because infections, failure of organs and so on will always be with us and because ill-health is a relative rather than absolute concept. As standards of health improve conceptions of what constitutes sickness change. In many ways the welfare

state has been very successful in its attempts to improve general levels of health. The battle against infectious diseases in particular has progressed well:

> Over the past thirty years, there have been dramatic reductions in the prevalence of a number of infectious diseases ... Diphtheria and acute poliomyelitis have almost been eradicated in this period. However, certain other infectious diseases can and do recur[69]

The NHS can take credit for this success as it is partially due to its vaccination schemes. Improvements in general living conditions are also part of the reason, though. Many other health problems have been successfully tackled so that the general mortality rate has fallen, increasing life expectancy.

Mortality Trends in the United Kingdom

	1951	1979/80
Expectation of Life from Birth (years):		
Males	66.2	70.2 (1979)
Females	71.2	76.2 (1979)
Infant mortality (a)	32	11.2 (1980)
Perinatal mortality (b)	39	12.8 (1980)
Maternal mortality (c)	80	14 (1979)

(a) Deaths of infants under one year of age per 1,000 live births
(b) Still births and deaths of infants under one week of age per 1,000 live and still births
(c) Rate per 100,000 live and still births[70]

However, this generally positive picture of the effects of health policy is qualified by the inequalities in health and health care provision across the social classes, geographically and in different areas of the work of the NHS.

Looking at inequalities in health across the social classes, the Black Report on the social distribution of health, (the findings of the Working Party set up by the 1974-1979 Labour government) clearly shows that the lower social classes are more prone to most types of illness than the upper. The government's own General Household Survey shows that, especially for males, people in social class V suffer particularly badly from digestive diseases and cancers of the stomach compared to those in social class I. Diseases of the urinary system, respiratory system and the circulatory system are also considerably higher for men in social class V than social class I, with a fairly clear class gradient between them.[71] In terms of mortality, there is a clear increasing trend in the death rate as one moves down the social scale. In 1971 the death rate for social class

I males was 3.98 per 1,000 of the population aged 15-64 years, for social class V males it was 9.88. For females the respective figures were 2.15 and 5.31. In 1980 the perinatal mortality rate for class I was 9.7, for class V it was 17.0. In that year the infant mortality rate was 8.9 for class I and 16.0 for class V. [72]

Have these inequalities by social class been reduced over the years; can we expect them to disappear in some years' time? Reliable figures on morbidity (sickness) by social class over the years are not available, and they would probably show different characteristics for different diseases. Mortality figures *are* available by social class over a lengthy time span and they indicate that while there has been a reduction for all socio-economic groups this reduction has been most marked in the upper sections. This has led to a widening of socio-economic inequalities in terms of mortality over the years even though there has been a substantial reduction in mortality rates for all social classes.

Socio-economic group of men aged 20-64 and standardised mortality ratios, England and Wales

Socio-Economic Group	1921-3	1930-2	1949-53	1959-63	1970-2
Professional	82	90	86	76	77
Managerial and lower professional	94	94	92	81	81
Skilled Manual	95	97	101	100	104
Semi-skilled Manual	101	102	104	103	113
Unskilled Manual	125	111	118	143	137

Geographical inequalities in NHS health provision are quite marked. Inner city areas, especially those in London, have inferior medical services in terms of GP's and surgeries. Nationally there is an inverse correlation between the health needs of the population and the provision they receive so that poor areas, especially in the north of the country, have fewer hospitals, GP's and so on relative to their needs. [74] Despite attempts to improve this situation in the 1970's the inequalities remain almost as great as they were on the Appointed Day in 1948.

With respect to inequalities of provision within the NHS by type of care, it is well known that two sectors suffer in terms of funding, quality of buildings and qualifications held by the staff in them. These are the geriatric sector of the service and the provision for the mentally ill and handicapped. Even though 53 per cent of hospital beds are occupied by the mentally ill and handicapped only 25 per cent of the total hospital budget is spent on their care. During the last twenty years, however, there has been an effort to take geriatric and the mentally ill and handicapped cases out of the hospitals and into the care of the local social services departments. Government figures show that in 1981, 7.9 per 1,000 of the elderly were in geriatric hospitals and 18 per 1,000 in local authority residential establishments compared to 9.4 and 14 in 1960. The proportion of mentally handicapped adults per 1,000 of the general population in hostels and homes compared to hospitals was 0.28 and 0.9 respectively in 1981. The figures were 0.03 and 1.3 in 1965 and 1961 respectively.

Ignorance
On the surface the history of the effects of education policy is a happy one. Attendance at school by the under fives, expressed as a percentage of the population aged 3-4 years, increased from 15 per cent in 1966 to 44.3 per cent in 1981, though the figure for 1982 fell (for the first time since 1966) to 42.8 per cent because of limits on local government expenditure.[75] More young people are entering full time further education and higher education now. Expressed as a percentage of all school leavers, 19.5 per cent of boys and 24.1 per cent of girls continued their education in these sectors in 1970/1, while the respective figures for 1981/2 were 23.7 per cent and 32.8 per cent.[76] DES statistics show that pupil-teacher ratios fell in both primary and secondary schools between 1950 and 1979 (from 31.0 to 23.1 for primary and 21.2 to 16.7 for secondary). How far the education system is improving in its attempts to educate young people is difficult to measure. A DES study on the reading abilities of 11 year olds found a rising trend in reading standards between 1955 and 1976-7. After a review of the sparse evidence available on standards in education V George and P Wilding conclude that not only is there no cause for concern but that there have been some improvements over the years.[77] The problems that exist in education are not to do with *minimum* standards but *relative* standards and what schools *could* achieve were it not for underfunding and, recently, the cuts in education expenditure imposed by the 1979-84 Conservative governments. *Origins and Destinations* by A H Halsey et al[78] offers considerable evidence on the relative achievements in education of different social classes using information obtained from a survey of 10,000 men in England and Wales conducted in 1972. They found that children of what they call 'the service class' (higher and lower grade professionals, administrators and managers, proprietors, supervisors and higher grade technicians, together amounting to 13.4 per cent of their total sample) were ten times more likely to still be at school at the age of 18 years than children of the working class (skilled, semi and unskilled manual workers, agricultural workers and smallholders.) Less

than 2.5 per cent of children in the working class gained the Higher School Certificate or an 'A' level pass, compared to 25 per cent from the service class.[79] Just over 10 per cent from the working class got the School Certificate or one or more 'O' levels, compared with over 50 per cent of the service class and 25 per cent of the children of the intermediate class (clerical, sales and service workers, small proprietors and self-employed artisans, lower grade technicians and foremen).[80]

The higher one goes in education, then, the more one finds service class children in proportion to children of the working class.

The Class Composition of Successive Stages of Educational Selection
(percentages)

Father's Social class	Selective Secondary Schools	O-Levels	A-Levels	University
I, II (service class)	27.4	35.5	49.1	52.4
III, IV, V (intermediate class)	34.9	34.2	29.4	27.9
VI, VII, VIII (working class)	37.7	30.2	21.5	19.7
All	100.0	99.9	100.0	100.0[81]

On the basis of the evidence collected in their comprehensive study, Halsey et al conclude:

> In summary, school inequalities of opportunity have been remarkably stable over the forty years which our study covers. Throughout, the service class had roughly three times the chance of the working class of getting some kind of selective secondary schooling. Only at sixteen has there been any significant reduction in relative class chances, but even here the absolute gains have been greater for the service class[82]

Just as the education system favours the middle class and wastes the talents of working class children, so it distinguishes between the two sexes, favouring the male, though this difference is less marked than the socio-economic one. V George and P Wilding write:

> The ratio of girls to boys going to university fluctuated from 70 per cent in 1925; 50 per cent in 1937; 47 per cent in 1950; 50 per cent in 1960; 66 per cent in 1973; and it has remained at that level since. The position of the two sexes has been the exact opposite in relation to further education, and to teacher training. In both these areas of higher education women have always outnumbered men. The ratio of boys to girls going on to further education was 50 per cent

in 1925, and 63 per cent in 1978. The figure for teacher training were 32 per cent and 26 per cent respectively[83]

Within school, DES figures suggest that while girls take and get more 'O' levels than boys and more often take and get one or two 'A' levels, they are less likely to get three 'A' levels. It is well known that certain subjects within the school curriculum are concentrated on predominantly by one sex or the other, and this suggests wastage of the talent of members of the other sex in these areas. Overall, though, George and Wilding conclude that substantial progress has been made in the last twenty years in relation to reduction of sex inequalities in education.

A third group who suffer educational disadvantage in public education are the children of ethnic minority groups, particularly West Indians. The Rampton Committee set up by the Labour government in 1979 to look into the education of ethnic minority groups published an interim report on their findings in 1981. The following table comes from that report.

Educational Achievements of Children of Ethnic Minority Groups in six LEAs 1978/9 (percentages)

Ethnic Group	'A' level pass		Destination of school leavers			
	None	One or More	University	Other F.E.	Employment	Not Known
Asians	87	13	3	18	54	25
West Indians	98	2	1	16	65	18
All School Leavers	88	12	3	9	77	11
All maintained School leavers in England	87	13	5	14	74	8 [84]

It seems that the educational provision of the British welfare state leaves a considerable amount to be desired for the children of the working class and of ethnic minority groups. However, in terms of absolute levels of provision its achievements have been considerable.

Squalor
The effects that housing policy has had since the Second World War represents the greatest success story of the five giants, at least in absolute terms. The number of dwellings in the UK increased from 14 million in 1951 to 21.84 million in 1982. .The number of dwellings available exceeded the number of households in 1961 and the gap between them has increased since so that there were almost 2 million more dwellings

than households in 1982. This does not mean that everyone who wants a home has one. Some dwellings are in areas where there is no demand, others are second homes of the middle class, some are empty. Homelessness still exists especially in urban areas and particularly in the inner city areas of London. Exactly what its extent is cannot be established because as well as finding temporary accommodation and accommodation with statutory and voluntary bodies, many of the homeless do not appear in official statistics as they are put up by relatives and friends. The National Dwelling and Housing Survey estimated 253,000 concealed households of this type in Britain in 1977, though the figure must be approximate. Local authorities can evade their responsibilities by adopting a strict interpretation of the clause in the 1977 Housing Act which relieves them of responsibility for people who could have foreseen their homelessness:

> Many people who are homeless as a result of family disputes, rent arrears and other such social and economic reasons are treated by many councils as intentionally homeless and are refused housing[85]

Despite this the number of homeless families housed by local authorities in England has risen from 33,600 in 1975 to 70,010 in 1981, with another 840,000 households on council waiting lists around the country.

The quality of the housing stock has, meanwhile, been improving. In 1951 there were 7.5 million households in unfit or sub-standard housing. In 1976 the figure was 1.65 million, most of these being in innner city areas, particularly in London, Scotland and the North of England. The table opposite shows some of the improvements in the housing stock by type of tenure.

This generally rosy picture is qualified when we look at relative access to high quality housing across the social classes. Even though house ownership has increased since the war the majority of working class people still live in council or other rented accommodation. This means that they suffer the low esteem of living in council estates and do not benefit from the tax concessions available to house purchasers. Neither do they receive the advantages of the profits to be made from house purchase. A house bought in 1949 worth £800 was worth £12,000 in the 1960's and £50,000 in the early 1980's. The only advantage to be gained from being a poor council tenant is housing benefit. The working class are more likely to suffer overcrowding and to have fewer amenities such as sole use of bath/shower and water closet or having central heating. The 1979-84 Conservative government's policy of selling council houses to those tenants who wish to buy them has meant that much of the higher quality council housing is no longer available to groups in need of

Housing standards by tenure, Great Britain (percentage)

| | Lacking sole use of | | | | without central heating | |
| | Bath/shower | | w/c inside building | | | |
	1971	1982	1971	1982	1971	1982
All owner occupiers	7	2	9	2	51	29
Rented from local authorities/new town	3	1	5	2	76	48
Rented privately						
unfurnished	33	13	37	12	85	63
furnished	58	37	57	37	83	69
All tenures	12	3	13	4	66	40

86

Ethnic Group and Housing Conditions, England 1979 (percentages)

	Ethnic Group of Head of Household					All Households
	White	West Indian	African	Indian/ Pakistan Bangladeshi	Other	
Tenure						
Owner-occupied	54.6	35.9	22.6	69.9	48.3	54.4
Council rented	30.0	45.2	29.0	10.1	18.0	29.8
Other rented	15.4	18.8	48.4	20.0	33.7	15.7
At least one basic amenity lacked	5.8	4.6	2.4	11.5	5.4	5.8
Pre 1919 property	26.6	46.8	58.9	61.7	39.7	27.3
Two or more below standard	0.5	2.2	2.3	8.3	2.6	0.6

87

council accommodation. These people are even more likely now to suffer the problems of damp, poor quality housing which no-one wants to buy. This fact indicates that it is misleading to discuss the working class as a whole. Those who can afford to buy their council houses are in an advantageous position compared to the poorest sectors. Certain ethnic groups within the working class are particularly disadvantaged in terms of housing, particularly those of Asian origin. These problems have not been eased by the fact that the annual rate of construction of council houses dropped by one third between 1976 and 1982.

To conclude this section we can, on the positive side, say that:

housing conditions measured in traditional ways (by counting rooms and persons per room, indoor toilets and plumbing fixtures) have since the Second World War grown better and more equal[88]

However inequalities do remain and will continue to do so, of course, as long as income inequalities remain.

Idleness

If housing is a success story in absolute terms at least, the effects of social policy on unemployment are the reverse. The rate of unemployment was low in the 1950's and 1960's. It oscillated around the 3 per cent level, never going above 5 per cent and often falling below 3 per cent (Beveridge's minimum possible.) The mid 1970's saw a change, however, with the level rising above 5 per cent, staying around that level and then sharply climbing in 1979/80:

Unemployment rate, percentages UK

1976	1977	1978	1979	1980	1981	1982
5.5	5.8	5.7	5.3	6.8	10.5	12.2 [89]

The number of unemployed in October 1984 was 3.25 million people, representing 12½ per cent of the workforce. These are official figures, however, based on those eligible to claim unemployment benefit only, thus excluding unemployed married women for example. Unofficial figures suggest something more like 4 million unemployed.

Unemployment is almost twice as likely to occur to men as women, at least according to official figures, and almost twice as likely to affect those under 19 than those above it (taken as a complete group.) West Indian, Bangladeshi and Pakistans workers have a rate of unemployment just over 20 per cent, while young male members of these groups have unemployment rates in the region of 37 per cent. In terms of area of the country, Northern Ireland has the highest level of unemployment, (19.4 per cent in 1982,) the South East has the lowest (8.7 per cent in 1982.) Central urban areas such as Liverpool, Newcastle and Manchester have rates around 30 per cent. The government's attempts to create and retain jobs do not appear to have been successful. It is difficult to measure the number of jobs created by government schemes. They are often temporary or merely replace a job which already existed with an MSC funded one. Whatever the actual figure is it clearly falls well short of Beveridge's aim. The government argues that in a world recession it is impossible to artificially create jobs without severe disruption to the economy and Britain's competitiveness. Many Marxists believe that the government is deliberately creating high levels of unemployment in order to reduce wage levels and curtail union power. Let us now consider in detail the response of each of the social policy perspectives to the developments in the welfare state since 1945.

The perspectives' response to the effects of welfare measures

For Social Democrats the inadequacies in the various sectors of the welfare state we have highlighted are not surprising. They reflect the weak commitment which successive governments have had to resolving the problems of those in need and unwillingness to spend money on doing so.

With respect to poverty, Social Democrats generally see this as a product of the poverty trap and/or the too-hierarchical nature of our society. They do not see this as the result of a culture of poverty among the poor which inculcates norms and values that keep them poor (immediate gratification, anti-educational attitudes, laziness.) The poverty trap means that the effect of social policy has been to make it very difficult to get *out* of poverty once one is in it. One of the most significant parts of it is the decline in tax thresholds which has meant that even the poor have to pay tax on their earnings. Paradoxically, being poor is comparatively expensive. The poor live in draughty houses which cost a lot to heat, they do not have access to cheap shops because they lack transport. They spend a larger proportion of their income on indirect taxation than the rich do. The stigma attached to means-tested benefits especially makes it difficult to re-enter the normal world once one has fallen on hard times. Often there are insufficient funds for clothes, travel and other expenses associated with finding another job.

The critique of the hierarchical nature of our society is a related, though more radical approach to the question of poverty. This argues that those at the top of the stratification system have been allowed to accumulate rewards for themselves, such as high incomes, excessive wealth and long holidays. Those at the bottom, lacking power, have had to pay for these benefits, particularly the dependents of those in work who receive little or nothing from the state or anyone else. These inequalities are aggravated by a society which imposes innumerable wants on people (cars, televisions, washing machines) which they can ill-afford but which they are encouraged to buy to ensure bouyant consumption levels. This casts the poor into even deeper debt. Peter Townsend in *Poverty in the United Kingdom* adopts this approach.

From the Social Democratic perspective, the governments of the last four decades have not fully addressed these problems. Much more generous and universalistic provision is necessary to eliminate the poverty trap. This would involve substantial redistribution of incomes. To reduce the inequalities in society would require more radical measures. Peter Townsend recommends:

1. Abolition of excessive wealth.
2. Abolition of excessive income.
3. Breaking down the distinction between earners and dependents.
4. Abolition of unemployment (by the obligation on authorities to provide work.)
5. Reorganisation of employment and professional practice (to restrict the power of professional and other groups.)
6. Reorganisation of community service (to make members of the community, rather than government departments, responsible for the old, the disabled and the mentally ill. [90]

The charge of 'too little too late' also applies to the health service. Writing from a Social Democratic perspective Dr Julian Tudor Hart, the originator of the inverse care law (which states that health resources are inversely correlated with need) comments that:

> If the National Health Service had continued to adhere to its original principles, with construction of health centres a first priority in industrial areas, all financed from taxation rather than direct flat-rate contribution, free at the time of use, and fully inclusive of all personal health services, including family planning, the operation of the Inverse Care Law would have been modified much more than it has been ... The force that creates and maintains the Inverse Care Law is the operation of the market, and its cultural and ideological superstructure which has permeated the thought and directed the ambitions of our profession ... The more health services are removed from the force of the market, the more

successful we can be in redistributing care away from its 'natural' distribution in a market economy[91]

Failures in education, housing and employment initiatives similarly result from the willingness of the government to allow the free market to operate alongside state intervention, even encouraging the former at the expense of the latter. Whilst most Social Democrats do not wish to see the total elimination of private enterprise and the free market, preferring as they do a mixed system, they call for far more restraints on the market than have so far been imposed and much more positive discrimination towards the poor.

From a *Marxist* perspective this failure of government is not surprising. Operating as it is within a capitalist system and being very much the tool of the bourgeoisie, government can do little to restrict the free market or make society more equal. It cannot solve the structural contradictions within capitalism. The replacement of people by machines in the workplace will inevitably happen due to the need to remain competitive and thus *must* create unemployment. Low wages, and therefore poverty, are inevitable in a society based upon the search for maximum profits. Disease which results from bad environmental conditions at home and at work combined with poor diet also is the consequence of a socio-economic system which places profitability before health considerations. Inequalities in education must result from a system which has the aim of reproducing an unequal class structure rather than providing true equality of opportunity.

Structuralists in general, reject individualists' claims that deliberate attempts to change arrangements within a given socio-economic structure, or mode of production, can have any important effect. To implement Townsend's suggestions within capitalism would mean a destruction of work incentives so that capitalists would find it difficult to recruit labour. Any attack on wealth distribution would see a flight of capital abroad and this would undermine the British economy. As long as the welfare state is restricted to aiding capitalism through the provision of minimum standards, paid for by the working class, then there are no problems. This, for the Marxist, is what it has done since its inception and it has largely been successful in maintaining the stability of capitalism. As soon as any attempt is made to go beyond the provision of minimum standards to ones which reduce inequalities in society and threaten profits and the privileged position of the few then a reaction would begin. However, according to Nicos Poulantzas[92] the interests of governments and of the capitalist class are so inextricable as to make such an attempt unlikely. The government aims at a healthy, internationally competitive economy. This implies low wage levels, low inflation and high levels of profitability (and therefore reinvestment.) To direct resources away from this objective into an overblown welfare state or into an attempt to remove the conditions which produce ill health (pollution, dangerous working conditions, environmental hazards, poor diets) would be to undermine our economic viability as a capitalist economy. The two aims are incompatible. For this reason it is not surprising that trends in wealth ownership have been towards greater inequalities since 1979. In 1982 the richest quarter of the population owned 81 per cent of all marketable wealth compared to 77 per cent in 1979, according to *Inland Revenue Statistics 1984*. These increasing inequalities are largely due to the gradual dismantling of taxation of capital. [93] Serious attacks on private education and on inequalities within the state education system are prevented, partially at least, by the predominance of ex public-school boys in government and the civil service. This is demonstrated by Ralph Miliband in his *The State in Capitalist Society*. Far from removing inequalities, then, the welfare state creates the circumstances which allow the perpetuation of inequality. Minor redistribution within the working class through the provision of benefits and services serves to placate that class.

Functionalists, like Marxists, see the social structure as imposing limits on what can be done through social policy initiatives. Insofar as the institutions of the welfare state perform the functions required of them, they can be said to have achieved their aims. Functionalists do not see the reduction of inequalities of wealth and income as necessary, in fact such reduction can be dysfunctional. K Davis and W E Moore[94] argue that differential rewards in society ensure that the most able have an incentive to fight to achieve top positions so that society can attain its goals more effectively. H Gans, also a functionalist, suggests that the existence of poverty at the *bottom* of the social scale is also functional. [95] It motivates people to do dirty menial jobs, creates jobs in a number of professions, ensures that old, shoddy goods are bought, allows expression of righteousness through charity and guarantees the high status of those not in poverty. The role of the welfare state is to eliminate the *absolute* poverty which might cause social disintegration, to provide a minimum of social rights. As we have seen it has largely done this.

There are improvements still to be made in the working of the welfare state. The figure of nearly 3 million below the official poverty line indicates inadequacies in the system. Large scale unemployment, especially among young and black people, may lead to marginalisation of these groups. Such social disintegration may lead to riots and other manifestations of social unrest such as those which occurred in the summer of 1981 in London and Liverpool. Dysfunctions within the education system mean that it is not performing its role of selecting the best brains to fill the top jobs. The talent of the working class, of black ethnic minorities and of girls is being lost to the community. The inadequacy of proper health care facilities for some sectors of the community means that these people are not operating at full efficiency and this too is dysfunctional for society. Resources should be orientated in the direction of the young and temporarily incapacitated and away from those who can no longer contribute to the working of society such as the old and disabled.[96] On the whole, the continued functioning of British society without severe disruption indicates that the welfare state has performed its role well.

For Market Liberals the evidence we have reviewed indicates that the welfare state has done more than we should require of it. It has ensured that virtually everybody is above the subsistence level, has provided health care facilities for those too poor to pay for them, provided a good standard of primary, secondary and further education for all and ensured that those genuinely in need of housing can get it. It has, however, gone too far in this. Unemployment is now no longer something to be avoided at all costs: the state will cushion the blow. This has led to demands for higher wages and a readiness to become unemployed which would not occur under laissez-faire capitalism. Incentives to work hard have been curtailed by high levels of taxation. Thus we find the high levels of unemployment and reduction in the general profitability of industry which has characterised the British economy recently.

Market Liberals applaud the actions of the 1979-1984 Conservative governments in reducing expenditure on many areas of the welfare state and generally attempting to bring the laws of supply and demand into its operation. Increases in charges for prescriptions will limit demand for drugs which, being over-subsidised in the past, were over-prescribed and so a burden on the tax payer. The abolition of wage-related unemployment benefit (in 1982) means that unemployment is a less attractive proposition than before. The same is true of the taxation of social security benefits in 1982. The obligation that local councils now have to sell their houses to tenants who wish to buy means that more people will be able to enjoy the advantages and pleasures of house ownership and will work harder and longer to maintain and improve their property. The suspension of supplementary benefit payments to workers on strike, in 1980, has reduced the number of strikes and shortened their duration. The government's attempts to reduce bureaucracy in the social services by closing a number of Job Centres, will reduce a burden on public expenditure and shift these unproductive workers into the wealth creating manufacturing industries. Reductions in public expenditure will enable taxes to be reduced, thus increasing work incentives and giving people more spending power. In turn this will fuel the economy to higher levels of productivity and profitability. Privatisation of many public-sector services (catering and cleaning within hospitals) will increase efficiency and further reduce the burden on the tax payer. To summarise, the Market Liberal sees the welfare state as having gone too far. A minimum level of state intervention is necessary to help those who cannot help themselves. Previous governments, pushed by interested pressure-groups, have been swayed into over-generous policies which have undermined wealth-creation, encouraged strikes and high wages, discouraged hard work and fuelled inflation. Recent governments have come under the influence of Market Liberals in the academic world (notably Friedman and Hayek) and have seen the error of this course. The balance is now being redressed and the resources of the welfare state are being concentrated on those few who need them.[97]

The Welfare State and Social Inequality

It is clear from the evidence that the welfare state has not eliminated inequalities in education, health, income or housing. Each of the perspectives tends to believe that its existence has helped to *reduce* inequality. The Social Democrat R H Tawney has referred to the Strategy of Equality by which he means the achievement of social and economic equality through public spending on social services. Taxing the rich and giving to the poor through provision of services. Most of the other Social Democrats such as A Crosland and R H Crossman agree that this is the effect of the welfare state, though not Peter Townsend. Market Liberals concur, arguing that the process of equalisation has gone too far. Most Marxists believe that the working class are the main recipients of public expenditure and that this fact helps to pacify them, gives them a stake in the capitalist system and makes them into healthy and efficient workers. Likewise functionalists believe that by giving benefits to the poorest the needs of the whole social system are served best and that this is one of the functions of the welfare state.

This virtual unanimity on the effect of the welfare state may be misfounded however. In this section we will examine the overall impact of the existence of the welfare state on social inequality. This will be done by asking two questions: who pays most for the welfare state and who receives most in benefits from it.

Who pays most for the Welfare State?

Welfare benefits are largely paid for from taxation. This takes different forms and may be progressive (the rich pay more) or regressive (the poor pay more, at least as a percentage of their total income.) *Income* tax aims at being progressive by:

(a) allowing part of a person's income to be tax free so that the lower paid have a smaller proportion of their income taxed than do the higher paid.

(b) having graduated tax rates, ranging from the lowest rate at 30 per cent to 60 per cent for those on high incomes (1984 figures).

With regard to (a) the point at which income tax begins to be levied (the tax threshold) is very low, so that even the low paid are caught in the tax net. Frank Field[98] has shown that the tax threshold has fallen as a percentage of average earnings since 1949-50. In that financial year a single person started paying tax at a little below 40 per cent of average earnings. In 1978-79 this had fallen to 21.8 per cent. The figures for a married couple were 63 per cent and 34 per cent respectively:

> Over the years more and more people have been called upon to pay direct (income) tax and consequently the number of tax paying units jumped from 13.5 million in 1945 to 21.3 million in 1978-79[99]

With regard to (b) Field points out that there is a very wide range of incomes on the basic rate of taxation so that the relatively well off and the relatively poor are paying the same rate. The degree of progressiveness of income tax in this respect was reduced by the 1979 (Conservative) budget which reduced the top rate of income tax from 83 per cent to its present 60 per cent. It also raised the threshold at which higher rate of tax became payable.

With regard to income tax, we can say that it *is* progressive but it has become less so over time. Analysing the effects of the 1979 and 1980 budgets, Field concludes:

> From the 1979 budget changes the poorest 10 per cent of taxpayers, for example, gained only 2 per cent of the £4.6 billion reduction in taxation. In contrast, the richest 1 per cent of taxpayers cornered 15 per cent of the total tax cuts and the top 7 per cent of taxpayers ... gained between them £1.6 billion, or 34 per cent of the tax handouts ... The overall effect of the 1980 budget was similar ...[100]

Another form of direct taxation is National Insurance contributions, now payable at 9 per cent of salary. This too is progressive, as the earlier flat rate contribution (abolished in 1966) was not. However it is payable on all income above £29.50 per week (1982-83 figure), so that the low threshold brings even the poor into the contribution scheme. There is also an upper limit (£220 per week in 1982-3) beyond which National Insurance contributions cease. This means that virtually all manual workers will pay the full contribution on all their earnings, whereas a substantial number of professional and managerial employees will escape having to contribute on a substantial part of their income.[101] Also National Insurance is only payable on earned income leaving income from rent, dividends and interest tax free in this respect. This too supports the thesis that the redistributive effects of taxation are limited.

Unlike direct (income) tax, indirect taxation (tax on goods, mainly VAT) is generally agreed to be regressive. Field points out that in 1979 only 2.5 per cent of the top 10 per cent's income went in VAT. 3.3 per cent and 3.1 per cent of the incomes of the ninth and tenth decile (the two poorest tenths in terms of income) went on VAT. He quotes a Department of Health and Social Security confidential minute, leaked to *The New Statesman,* which stated that:

> tax could be said to be progressive if the proportion of the disposable income of the poorer household which is paid in tax is lower than that of the richer household. On this measure, commodity taxation as it existed in 1977 was regressive[102]

In 1979 the rate of VAT was increased to 15 per cent, and an increasingly wide range of goods has been made liable to VAT by the Chancellor. Most recently this has involved the controversial measure of charging VAT on hot take-away food such as fish and chips. J C Kincaid points out that the employer's contribution to National Insurance should be seen as a tax on commodities like VAT, because employers simply add the cost of their contribution to the price of the goods they manufacture.[103]

Calculating the progressive effect of direct taxation and the regressive effect of indirect taxation, J Westergaard and H Resler conclude that those on the lowest income pay less in taxes than the rest. However, above this lowest level of income the tax burden remains about the same, regardless of total weekly income. Therefore the overall effect of taxation is hardly progressive at all.

Who benefits most from the Welfare State?

Most people, including academics who recognise that the poor pay disproportionately towards the cost of the welfare state, tend to assume that the poor benefit most from the money and services which it provides. Social Democrats like R M Titmuss and David Donnison believe this to be the case as far as *direct* state benefits are concerned. They note that the welfare state could also be said to include occupational benefits and fiscal social security, ie tax concessions. Occupational benefits include company cars, meals, pensions and private health subscriptions paid for by one's company. Indirectly, the state finances these through tax concessions to companies to offset their cost. Direct tax concessions to individuals, fiscal social security, include tax relief on mortgage interest payment (for home owners), life assurance relief (on policies taken out prior to April 1984), relief on bank loan interest payments and contributions to superannuation and retirement pensions and on fees to professional bodies. Assessing the effect of these benefits, Donnison writes:

> The occupational and fiscal welfare systems confer their biggest benefits on the rich, because employers are more generous to their top people and tax reliefs are worth more to those who pay a lot of tax [104]

Some writers maintain that even *direct* state benefits are used more by those in higher income groups and middle class occupations than by the poor and working class. Julian Le Grand in *The Strategy of Equality* [105] has made a detailed study of the idea that the welfare state promotes equality by benefiting the poor more than the rich. Studying the NHS in this respect he finds that the same amount is spent on each socioeconomic group. When one takes in to account the fact that the higher groups are healthier than the lower one finds that professionals, employers and managers receive up to 40 per cent more National Health Service expenditure *per ill person*. This is demonstrated in the table opposite.

The reasons for this inequality are numerous. Working class people find it difficult and expensive (in terms of money, time and effort) to take advantage of medical facilities. Doctors will be less sympathetic to them and give them less time. Medical facilities are not as plentiful in poor areas as in affluent ones. Doctors are less likely to refer working class patients to specialists. Working class people are more likely to lose pay if they take time off to visit doctors and hospitals. The most important reason is the extra costs in terms of effort, time, travel expenses and lost earnings which use of 'free' medical facilities have for a working class person than for a middle class one. The principal determinants of inequalities in the use of health care are beyond the

*Public Expenditure on Health care by Socio-economic Group,
England and Wales 1972*

ALL PERSONS Socio-economic group	Expenditure per person; percentage of mean	Expenditure per person reporting illness; percentage of mean

Professionals,
  employers and
  managers
	94	120.

Intermediate and junior non-manual	104	114
Skilled manual	92	97
Semi and unskilled manual	114	85
Mean (£)	18.1	103.2 [106]

control of the NHS, they:

> stem from basic social and economic inequalities, that is, the inequalities in income which lead to inequalities in car and telephone ownership; the differences in working conditions that leave some individuals free to attend the doctor without losing money, but others not; the class divisions that render different groups in society mistrustful of, and hostile to, each other. Inequality in health care reflects inequality in society. It seems that one cannot be altered without affecting the other[107]

In education, too, the rich benefit more. Public expenditure on compulsory education slightly favours the lower social groups while expenditure on post-compulsory education strongly favours the better off (with the possible exception of means-tested student grants):

> In Britain, the top fifth of the income distribution receives nearly three times as much public expenditure in education per household as the poorest fifth. If people are classified by occupation rather than income, a similar pattern appears, although not as pronounced. The top socio-cconomic group receives nearly 50 per cent more public expenditure per person in the relevant age range than the bottom group. This arises because, although they receive slightly less on primary and secondary education for pupils under 16, they receive substantially more on educating children over that age: twice as much for secondary pupils over 16, three times as much on further education, and over five times as much on university education[108]

The reasons why working class children tend to leave school early are again related to cost, this time the cost in terms of satisfaction or pleasure forgone by staying in education:

> Since it is reasonable to assume that each pound forgone represents a greater sacrifice for those from low income than those from high income families, the same (or even smaller) money costs for the former are likely to be a more important barrier to education than for the latter[109]

In housing, the:

> Direct expenditure on council housing favours the poor since they have a higher proportion of council tenants and because, due to the rate rebate system (now called housing benefit), poorer tenants receive a larger subsidy than richer ones. But, with the exception of rent allowances to private tenants, other areas of housing expenditure are basically pro-rich. Of these the most significant are tax expenditures, that is, the variety of different tax reliefs for owner-occupiers. Since owner-occupation is far more prevalent in the higher income groups, and since these tax expenditures increase with the tax rate faced by a household and with the size of its mortgage (both of which are generally higher for the wealthy) the distribution is markedly pro-rich, to such an extent that it more than offsets the pro-poor distribution of council housing. As a result the net effect is that, overall, public expenditure on housing favours the better off, with the highest group receiving nearly twice as much as the lowest[110]

In expenditure on transport, too, the rich do best. The highest income group benefit ten times as much per household from subsidised rail travel and seventeen times as much from the provision of roads. The distribution of public expenditure on bus travel appears to benefit more those higher up the social scale in terms of income but lower down in terms of occupation, though this area is less clear. All in all, however, it seems reasonable to assert that public expenditures on transport have not promoted equality in final income.[111]

Weighing up all the evidence on the effect of the welfare state on social inequality Julian Le Grand argues that it has increased rather than decreased it. This is despite the presence of benefits which are pro-poor such as public housing, housing benefit, means-tested benefit in the education sector and all programmes that are confined by policy decision to people on low income (supplementary benefit and family income supplement.) Peter Townsend agrees, finding that the income received by the richest 20 per cent is nearly four times that of the poorest 20 per cent.[112]

J Westergaard and R Resler concur, though they believe that the *very* poorest do receive a net gain from the state benefits. Frank Field also supports Le Grand's conclusion and rejects the government's view, as articulated by the Central Statistical Office, that the welfare state performs a 'Robin Hood' function:

> The official analysis of the Central Statistical Office offers an attempt to shore up the belief in the redistributive impact of the tax and benefit 'welfare state'. Such a belief cannot be supported by the evidence[113]

What policy implications do these findings have? The logical conclusion would appear to be that the best way to attack inequality in society would either be to dismantle the welfare state or to introduce much more means-testing of benefits. This is paradoxical for these are precisely the policies advocated by Market Liberals who have no interest in reducing inequality! Le Grand, though, rejects them both. The dismantling option might halt the distribution of benefits to the well off, but it would not necessarily help the poor unless the revenues saved were used specifically to improve their position. He considers that unlikely. The extension of means testing would suffer all the disadvantages which we discussed on pages 108-109. Le Grand argues that the inequalities in use of welfare benefits like health, education and transport stem from inequalities in income and wealth in society which enable the better off to take fullest advantage of these benefits. The best way to reduce inequality is to tackle it *directly,* not by the 'back door' method of providing benefits and services. The rich in every society are not only rich, they are also powerful. They can mobilise support in a number of directions if their position of privilege is attacked:

> They can buy media outlets which offer a view of the world which reinforces the ideology of inequality; they can threaten or actually undertake activities which undermine any attempt to deprive them of their wealth (by, say, firing troublesome workers, or emigrating to tax havens); and in extremis they can buy armies or police forces to defend them[114]

An aggressive attack on inequality will not work. What is necessary is a challenge to the *ideology* of inequality which precedes a challenge to inequality itself. It must be demonstrated to people that the poor have little control over their situation, that they are not to blame in any sense for being deprived. Factors beyond the control of individuals such as lack of jobs, difficulty of obtaining a good education for children of deprived backgrounds have led to their current situation. This will show to people, particularly the rich, that the current inequalities in society are not fair in any sense. Realising this the rich will be willing to redistribute their wealth. They will have been convinced by the force of ideas:

> ideology can override self-interest. People can be induced by ideology to perform all manner of bizarre activities that in no way further their own interests. Indeed, at the extreme, they can be persuaded to kill themselves in battle[115]

This is an idealist (as opposed to a materialist) view. For traditional Marxists it is naive in the extreme. A Marxist such as Louis Althusser would reply that the owning class would not allow such ideas to challenge bourgeois hegemony, which includes the idea of the rightness of inequality in society. Their control over the ideological state apparatus would ensure that such challenging ideas were rejected. If a successful ideological challenge *were* to be mounted they would not give away their wealth willingly. The forces of the state, the repressive state apparatus, would be called in to their defence. Some Marxists, such as Antonio Gramsci and modern Euro-communists would agree with Le Grand's position. They have more faith in the power of ideas than classical Marxism and do believe that one can successfully challenge bourgeois hegemony without the need for violent revolution. Social Democrats would accept Le Grand's view, indeed it is close to Townsend's position (dealt with on page 143.) Functionalists and Market Liberals reject the need to reduce inequalities in society to any great extent.

Sociology and Social Policy

The relationship between the academic discipline of sociology and social policy has always been a close one. The inventor of the word sociology, Anguste Comte, saw this discipline as:

> part of a determinate pattern of historical change. Once the sociologist had discovered laws of such change it was his task to use the discovery in order to mastermind the political course of 'social regeneration'[116]

Emile Durkheim, writing in the nineteenth century, also saw the role of sociology as the scientific investigation of social problems with a view to proposing policies to solve them. Thus for example high levels of suicide were seen as a manifestation of inadequate social integration in society.

To increase the levels of social integration social policy should be orientated to the setting up of communal work units and strengthening familial bonds (see page 72). More recent positivist sociology has avoided explicit concern with social policy, seeing the discipline as ideally value-free and hence uncommitted and non-judgemental. In its search for the facts and an understanding of an event in terms of the events which preceded it (if A occurs then B follows) it tries to avoid involvement in political issues. Academics, the theory goes, should venture out of their ivory towers only to conduct empirical investigation of the real world. Contact with politicians, commitment to political ideologies or concern about problems such as crime and poverty can only distort observation and blinker clear thought. If the findings of sociology are used by policy makers, that is a matter for them. If scientific studies of education demonstrate that there is a wastage of the talent of the working class, of immigrant groups and of girls under a particular educational system, then policy makers may want to use this information to justify change. However, encouraging change should not be the aim of the study otherwise bias will creep into its conduct.

Earlier in the book (page 64-66) we criticised the positivists' presumptions to value neutrality. Brian Fay provides a detailed criticism of the deliberate use to which positivist sociology can be put in social policy formulation.[117] He points out that if one seeks to understand an event in terms of the events which produce it, (as positivism does in its search for if A then B type laws) then one finds out how to produce B by simply arranging for A to happen in the right circumstances. He writes:

> The notion of understanding in science is intimately bound up with the notion of control, for it is our ability to control events, at least in principle, which constitutes one of the criteria in virtue of which one can be said to have given a valid scientific explanation[118]

It is therefore no accident that the earliest positivists were also deeply concerned with social policy. Fay adds, like Marcuse, that positivism is inherently conservative because it ignores alternative possibilities to that which exists. What doesn't exist can't be observed and is therefore ignored. It accepts current social relationships as necessarily the way they are, but treats individuals instrumentally to manipulate them so as to maximise their efficiency. For example, the economist J M Keynes describes how the capitalist system operates and then demonstrates how to improve it, especially in creating demand to reduce unemployment. But:

> The point here is that the so-called 'laws of the economic system'

are taken to be natural necessities like gravity, with the effect that the relationships which these laws describe are taken as given parameters within which the specified problem of unemployment must be solved. But this has the unwitting effect of reinforcing certain structural features of a particular form of industrial capitalism[119]

The *action* approach of phenomenology and interactionism does not manipulate people in this way. Instead it uses an interpretive method and so:

increases the *possibility of communication* between those who come into contact with the accounts of such a science and those whom it studies. For by revealing what it is that people are doing, ie by revealing the rules and assumptions upon which they are acting, it makes it possible for us to engage in a dialogue with them—we understand, as it were, the language of their social life[120]

This is illustrated by J Young's discussion of the drug-takers in Notting Hill and Thomas Gladwin on the Trukese navigators (page 28 and 35). Their actions are no longer perceived as inexplicable, irrational or arbitrary. In understanding others we also come to understand *ourselves* better by seeing ours not as *the* way of life but only one way. Unlike positivism, the action approach does not seek to explain the actions of a group, especially when this involves accounts which may not make sense to the group itself. A correct account has been given when the observer and the observed are talking about the actions and beliefs of the actor in the same way. However, there are problems with this approach too. Specifically, in concentrating on the microscopic level, action theory does not look at the structural conditions which may give rise to certain actions, values and beliefs. In studying the everyday life and attitudes of the poor we may miss the conditions within society which create poverty and the attitudes and lifestyle associated with it. This means too that structural conflict in society may be missed by the social scientist adopting this approach. Two other problems with it are that the sociologist *can* usefully explain things which are not apparent to the actor, particularly the unintended consequences of action which the latter may not connect to his/her behaviour. The church-goer may not appreciate that the ritual of church-going and worship is not only a religious act but also serves to reinforce social solidarity. It performs a function which the actor does not perceive but the sociologist, with a broader view, does. Finally the action approach cannot explain historical change. Like the functionalist approach it assumes *shared* meanings and thus can explain stasis but not change, except by invoking external forces.

In view of the problems associated with both the positivist and the action approaches, Fay suggests an alternative which he calls critical social science. This:

1. accepts the necessity of attempting to understand the motives for action and meanings about situations which the actor themselves have : hermeneutics.
2. accepts the dominance of structure over the individual so that actors have little or no control over the social conditions which constrain action. And,
3. is ... built on the explicit recognition that social theory is interconnected with social practice, such that what is to count as truth is partially determined by the specific ways in which scientific theory is supposed to relate to practical action.[121]

Critical theory ties its claims to possessing knowledge to what people actually *want,* which it has established through the interpretive method.

It is vital that such a social theory should not only *understand* the felt needs and sufferings, demonstrate the stuctural conditions which gave rise to them, but also should offer social policy solutions. It should show:

how these feelings can be overcome by the actors coming to understand themselves in their situation as the product of certain inherent contradictions in their social order, contradictions whch they can remove by taking an appropriate course of action to change their social order[122]

Policy makers may choose to reject these initiatives, but at least they would have to make a definite move to do so rather than arguing that the conservative policies which positivist sociology gives rise to are the only possible ones. The critical social scientist has *listened* to the views, needs and complaints of the people, understood them and the circumstances which created them. Proposals are then put.

How different all this is from the conception of a policy science developed out of the positivist model of social science. In that conception there is no requirement that the policy expert refer to the public expression of needs and wants ... In fact, a policy science is an elitist and anti-democratic programme designed to eliminate just those features of political decision-making which the critical model deems essential[123]

However it seems true that the more radical a study's social policy implications are the less likely it is to have an impact on social policy. Studies of poverty which adopt relative definitions of poverty or of ill-health tend largely to be ignored by governments because of the fundamental (and expensive) changes in social policy they imply. The Conservative government's rejection of the proposals contained in the Black report on inequalities in health illustrates this well. [124]

Bibliography

1 P Townsend *Sociology and Social Policy* Penguin, Harmondsworth 1975, p 6.
2 Ministry of Health *A National Health Service* CMND 6502 HMSO London 1944, p 5. Quoted in V George and P Wilding *The Impact of Social Policy* Routledge and Kegan Paul, London 1984, p 2.
3 This broad definition of social administration is a common theme among Social Democrats like Townsend. It is perhaps worth pointing out here that the term is used in two senses; as the actual implementation of social policy, and as the academic discipline which studies that implementation and the effects it has. Confusingly the Americans refer to the discipline as social policy. See, for example, M Rein *Social Policy: Issues of Choice and Change* Random House, New York 1970, p 3.
4 See V George and P Wilding *Ideology and Social Welfare* Routledge and Kegan Paul, London 1976 for a fuller discussion.
5 Many people believe that sociology is moving in this direction. At a time of educational cut-backs the grants available to researchers seem to increasingly conditional upon the relevance and usefulness of their work.
6 P Corrigan, in *Schooling the Smash Street Kids* Macmillan, London 1979 states that his view of the problem of education changed during the course of the study. From being working class failure in a generally benign system he later saw it as the imposition of middle class culture on a recalcitrant working class.
7 Individualism, or, more correctly, methodological individualism, is the doctrine which considers that explanations of complex social phenomena must be formulated in terms of or be reducible to the ations of individual human beings. See the glossary at the end of the knowledge chapter for definitions of other terms used here.
8 Asa Briggs *The Welfare State in Historical Perspective* European

Journal of Sociology, Vol 2, No 2, p 288. Piet Thoenes takes into account the socio-economic context within which the welfare state operates when he defines it as:

a form of society characterised by a system of democratic, government-sponsored welfare placed on a new footing and offering a guarantee of collective social care to its citizens, concurrently with the maintenance of a capitalist system of production.

P Thoenes   *The Elite in the Welfare State*   1966 p 125, quoted in W A Robson   *Welfare State and Welfare Society: Illusion and Reality*   George Allen and Unwin, London 1976 p 14.

9   W Beveridge   *Report on Social Insurance and Allied Services HMSO 1942 CMND 6404 p 170, paragraph 456.*

10   Some elements of the welfare state are omitted from this scheme too. Services for children and young people, the treatment of offenders, special services for the old and handicapped and other special groups (for example gypsies and vagrants) are not dealt with in detail. T H Marshall sees the following as the constituent elements of a welfare state: social security, health care, welfare, housing, community services, education. See T H Marshall *Social Policy*   Hutchinson, London   1975, first published 1965. Beveridge's scheme has the advantage of clarity, however. Social Democrats have suggested recently that transport should be seen as an element of the welfare state (see R Pinker   *Social Theory and Social Policy*   Heineman, London 1971) R M Titmuss suggests that fiscal and occupational benefits are also important elements.

11   W E Baugh   *Introduction to the Social Services*   Macmillan, London 1983 p 110.

12   Figure from J Mays et al (eds)   *Penelope Hall's Social Services of England and Wales*   R K P, London 1983 p 147. Local government finance comes from the rates, from charges for services (housing, leisure, libraries, allotments) and from the rate support grant. This latter makes up the difference between income and expenditure. The size of the Rate Support Grant is calculated by complicated formulae which have undergone many changes. Overall it has declined as a proportion of the average income of local authorities, from about 70 per cent to about 50 per cent between 1979 and 1983. This had to be made up elsewhere by local governments, particularly in view of the fines imposed for overspending.

13   Sunday Times 16 September 1984.

14   This is, of course, a highly contentious policy. Labour argues that

it reduces the stock of rented accommodation, used by the poor, and increases house ownership which is only available to those who can afford to pay.

15 The main reason for the changeover was to reduce administrative expenses for the Department of Health and Social Security as far as the rebates are concerned. Recent figures suggest that while the Department of Health and Social Security has managed to save money the scheme has cost Local Authorities even more as they have had to employ extra staff to administer the scheme, make payments and then claim the cost back from the Department of Health and Social Security.

16 D Donnison and C Ungerson *Housing Policy,* Penguin, Harmondsworth 1982 p 199.

17 For a fuller discussion of the welfare state students are directed to J Mays et al (eds) 1983 op cit. Much of the information in this section comes from this volume. W E Baugh's book (op cit) is also useful, if less detailed.

18 D Marsh *The Welfare State* Longman London 1980, first published 1970 pp 49-50. Industrial injury benefit has now been abolished.

19 Ibid p 58.

20. R M Titmuss *Essays on the Welfare State* George Allen and Unwin, London 1976 first published 1958 p 42.

21. See P Townsend 1975 op cit pp 3-5 for a fuller discussion of this point.

22. This is only one way of subdividing the perspectives. G Room in *The Sociology of Welfare* Basil Blackwell, Oxford 1979 distinguishes between the Neo-Marxist, Market Liberal, Political and Social Democratic approaches. V George and P Wilding in *Ideology and Social Welfare,* RKP, London 1976 refer to the Anti-Collectivists, Reluctant Collectivists, Fabian Socialists and Marxists: the first approximates to the Market Liberals, the second and third are combined here under the heading of Social Democrats. They have been criticised for exaggerating the reluctance of such 'Reluctant Collectivists' as Beveridge where state controlled social welfare measures are concerned.

23. G Room 1979 op cit. Others include C A R Crosland *The Future of Socialism,* Cape 1961, first published 1956, R H S Crossman *The Politics of Pensions,* Liverpool University Press, Liverpool 1972, R H Tawney *Equality,* Allen and Unwin, London 1964. These are V George and P Wilding's Fabian Socialists. Under the heading of Reluctant Collectivists they include W H Beveridge

Full Employment in a Free Society   Allen and Unwin, London 1944, J M Keynes   *The General Theory of Employment, Interst and Money,*   Macmillan, London 1946, first published 1936, and J K Galbraith   *The Affluent Society,*   Penguin, Harmondsworth 1962.

24. This list is derived from V George and P Wilding 1976 op cit.

25. W A Robson 1976 op cit p 34.

26. R M Titmuss   *The Gift Relationship,*   Allen and Unwin, London 1940 p 225.

27. Table adapted from R Mishra   *Society and Social Policy*   Macmillan, London 1984, first published 1977 p 101.

28. P Townsend 1976 op cit p 57.

29. Although R Pinker points out that some Social Democrats do not have an unqualified commitment to universalism—eg Titmuss. See R Pinker 1971 op cit p 100 C A R Crosland is another example.

30. Figures in W E Baugh op cit p 49: the figure of 80% comes from a parliamentary answer given in 1981.

31. W Beveridge   *Social Insurance and Allied Services*   1942 op cit p 12.

32. P Townsend 1976 op cit p 126.

33. See M Reddin   *Local Authority Means-Tested Services*   in P Townsend et al   *Social Services for All?*   Part One, Fabian Tract 38 pp 7-15 for examples of the increasing use of means testing by local authorities.

34. David Donnison, for example, in   *The Politics of Poverty* Robertson, London 1982 outlines the optimistic assumptions held by him and other Social Democrats mentioned here about the consensus held by all parties about welfare matters and their abilities to implement effective policies. He remarks, though, that 'Had we been more perceptive we would have noted the changes which were already eroding the economic and social structure on which this consensus rested.' p 22.

35. F A Hayek   *Individualism and Economic Order*   RKP, London 1949 p 23.

36. These points are based on comments in V George and P Wilding 1976 op cit.

37. Reported in The Guardian September 28, 1984.

38. M Friedman   *Capitalism and Freedom,*   Chicago University Press Chicago 1962 p 200. Quoted P Taylor Gooby and J Dale *Social Theory and Social Welfare,*   Edward Arnold, London 1981 p 61.

39. See F A Hayek   *The Constitution of Liberty,*   RKP, London

1960, p 229-230 for comments on this.

40. R Mishra 1984 op cit p 72.

41. H Westergaard *The Myth of Classlessness* in R Blackburn *Ideology in Social Science,* Fontana, London 1972 p 140.

42. Sir Ian Gilmour *Conservatism,* Lecture delivered at the Cambridge Union, 7 February 1980.

43. N Ginsberg *Class, Capital and Social Policy,* Macmillan, London 1979 p 47.

44. Ginsberg writes 'In a period of labour shortage married women may move into low-paid, short term employment outside the home, often part-time, and when they are no longer required, they can move quietly back into their families as full-time domestic workers. This has been encouraged by such policies as contracting out of National Insurance, the lack of substantial support in maternity, and the inappropriateness of the contribution principle in the context of women's intermittent employment outside the home.' N Ginsberg Ibid p 80.

    Non working women have always been treated as second class citizens by the social security system: in 1911 the National Health Insurance provided a flat rate payment, regardless of family size or whether one was married or single. It was nearly 40 years before the existence of a wife and children was recognised when a male worker became ill. Similarly when 'free' medical care by general practioners was introduced in 1913 it was only for insured workers and remained so until after the Second World War, the uninsured housewife had to look after herself

45. J Saville *The Welfare State: An Historical Approach* New Reasoner Vol 3 p 1957-8.

46. V George and P Wilding 1976 op cit p 104.

47. R Miliband in D Wedderburn (ed) *Poverty, Inequality and Class Structure* Cambridge University Press, Cambridge 1974 p 194.

48 R Titmuss 1976 op cit pp 43-4. His acknowledgements to E Durkheim are on pages 44 and 54.

49. R Titmuss ibid p 39 and *Commitment to Welfare,* Allen and Unwin, London 1968 p 191.

50. N Smelser *Toward a Theory of Modernisation,* quoted in R Mishra 1984 op cit p 56.

51. T H Marshall *Citizenship and Social Class* in T H Marshall *Sociology at the Crossroads and Other Essays,* Heineman, London 1963 (the essay was first published in 1950.) See T Parsons *The System of Modern Societies* Prentice Hall, Englewood Cliffs. 1971 p 81, 83, 93 and 94.

52. C Kerr et al *Industrialism and Industrial Man* Penguin, Harmondsworth 1973, first published 1960. The argument is summarised in R Mishra 1984 op cit pp 40-44.
53. R Mishra 1984 op cit p 42.
54. J Westergaard 1972 op cit pp 155-6.
55. N Ginsberg op cit p 40-41.
56. P Taylor Gooby and J Dale 1981 op cit pp 65-6.
57. K Marx *Marx Engels Gesamtausgabe* quoted in T B Bottomore and M Rubel (eds) *Karl Marx: Selected Writings in Sociology and Social Philosophy* Penguin, Harmondsworth 1973, first published 1956 p 179.
58. R M Titmuss 1976 op cit pp 38-9.
59. R Mishra 1984 op cit p 65.
60. V George and P Wilding *The Impact of Social Policy* RKP London 1984 pp 16-19.
61. P Townsend *Poverty in the United Kingdom* Penguin, Harmondsworth 1979.
62. See, for example, D Piachaud New Society 10 September 1981, pp 419-412. Townsend replies to these criticisms in New Society 17 September 1981, pp 447-478.
63. V George and P Wilding 1984 op cit p 23. Figures for each of the four years from (consecutively) B Abel-Smith and P Townsend *The Poor and The Poorest* Bell, 1965 p 58, Central Statistical Office (CSO) *Social Trends 1974,* HMSO 1974 table 80 p 123; CSO *Social Trends 1979* HMSO 1980; DHSS *Low Income Families* House of Commons Library October 1983.
64. See V George and P Wilding 1984 op cit p 21 Table 2.1 Figures based on Supplementary Benefits Commission Annual Report 1975 and 1979.
65. Ibid p 20.
66. P Townsend 1979 op cit p 273 Table 7.1 These figures are for the non-institutionalised population.
67. Royal Commission on the Distribution of Income and Wealth *Lower Incomes,* report no 6 CMND 7175, HMSO 1978 p 97-8. Quoted in V George and P Wilding 1984 op cit p 25.
68. S MacGregor *The Politics of Poverty* Longman, London 1981 p 41. The figures on social security expenditure are from the CSO's *Annual Abstract of Statistics* no 118, HMSO 1982, Table 3.1 p 56.
69. CSO *Social Trends 1984* no 14 HMSO, London 1984 p 99.
70. CSO *Social Trends 1982* quoted in V George and P Wilding 1984 op cit p 43.

71. See General Household Survey *Occupational Mortality 1970-1972* HMSO, London 1978.

73. Death rate figures from P Townsend and N Davidson *Inequalities in Health* Penguin, Harmondsworth 1982 p 57. Perinatal and infant mortality rates are from *Social Trends 1983,* HMSO London 1982 p 92.

73. Source J Brotherston *Inequality—Is it inevitable?* in C O Carter and J Peel (eds) *Equalities and Inequalities in Health* Academic Press 1976, Table 8.17. Cited in V George and P Wilding 1984 op cit p 90.

74. See J Tudor Hart *The Inverse Care Law* in the Lancet Vol 1 pp 405-12 1971. See P Trowler and M Riley *Topics in Sociology.* University Tutorial Press, Cambridge pp 179-184 for a fuller discussion of these points.

75. CSO *Social Trends 1984* HMSO, London Table 3.1 p 43.

76. Ibid p 48 Table 3.8.

77. V George and P Wilding 1984 op cit p 52.

78. A H Halsey, A F Heath and J M Ridge *Origins and Destinations* Clarendon Press, Oxford 1980.

79. Ibid p 204.

80. Ibid p 142.

81. Ibid p 185, table 10.6.

82. Ibid p 205.

83. V George and P Wilding 1984 op cit pp 73-4.

84. Interim Report of the Committee of Inquiry into the Education of Children from Ethnic Minority Groups *West Indian Children in Our Schools* CMND 8273, HMSO 1981, tables D and E, pp 8 and 9. Quoted ibid p 75.

85. V George and P Wilding 1984 op cit p 28.

86. Source CSO *Social Trends No 14 1984* Table 8.14 p 125.

87. DOE *National Dwelling and Housing Survey* HMSO, London 1979. Tabel 8, p 33. Cited in and adapted from V George and P Wilding 1984 op cit p 99. Bedroom standard means the number of bedrooms below the number required to give one to each married couple, one to each person over 21 years, and one per two people between 10 and 21 years of the same sex.

88. D Donnison and C Ungerson *Housing Policy* 1982 op cit p 18.

89. Source CSO *Social Trends 1984* op cit p 67 table 4.18.

90. P Townsend op cit p 926.

91. J T Hart op cit. Quoted in S Iliffe *The N.H.S. : A Picture of Health?* Lawrence and Wishart, London 1983 p 91.

92. See, for example, N Poulantzas *The Problem of the Capitalist*

State   in R Blackburn (ed) 1972 op cit pp 238-253.

93. Quoted in the *Guardian* 30 October 1984. The richest 1% owned 22% of marketable wealth in 1950, 21% in 1982, the richest ½ of the population owned 95% in 1979 and 96% in 1982. Capital Transfer Tax fell from 6.2% of all tax revenue in 1965-6 to 1.5% in 1979/80. This trend towards greater inequality reverses what was considered officially to be a trend in the opposite direction in post war years, though many academics have questioned that interpretation. See, for example, F Field   *Unequal Britain*   Arrow Books, London 1974, pp 57-61.

94 K Davis and W E Moore   *Some Principles of Stratification*   in R Bendix and S M Lipset (eds)   *Class Status and Power*   R K P London 1967.

95 H Gans   *The Positive Functions of Poverty,*   cited in P Townsend 1979 op cit p 85-7.

96. T Parsons implies this in   *The Social System*   RKP, London 1951 p 430 . . . 'illness incapacitates for the effective performance of social roles . . . there is a functional interest of the society in its control, broadly in the minimization of illness . . . From a variety of points of view, the birth and rearing of a child constitute a "cost" . . . Premature death, before the individual has had the opportunity to play act his full quota of social roles, means that only a partial "return" for this cost has been received.'

97. For a fuller exposition of the argument that social policy has undermined economic growth, and a critique of it, see V George and P Wilding 1984 op cit Chapter 5. Chapter 4 examines the view that social policy has actually *encouraged* economic growth.

98. F Field, M Meacher, Chris Pond   *To Him Who Hath*   Penguin Harmondsworth 1977.

99. F Field (ed)   *The Wealth Report 2*   RKP, London 1983 pp 57 and 58.

100. Ibid pp 62-3.

101. J C Kincaid   *Poverty and Equality in Britain*   Penguin, Harmondsworth 1975, first published 1973, p 93.

102. Quoted in F Field 1983 op cit p 67.

103. See J C Kincaid 1975 op cit p 81. He quotes a government report of 1969 which makes the same point.

104. D Donnison   *The Politics of Poverty*   op cit p 12. In the mid 1970's the senior management received 36% of their salaries plus bonus and commission *again* through superannuation and fringe benefits paid to them. See P Townsend New Society 7 October 1982 p 22.

105. Julian Le Grand *The Strategy of Equality* George Allen and Unwin London 1982.
106. Ibid p 26 table 3.1
107. Ibid p 51.
108. Ibid p 127.
109. Ibid p 63.
110. Ibid p 128.
111. Ibid p 117.
112. P Townsend 1979 op cit p 228 table 5.29.
113. F Field 1977 op cit p 201. The CSO's analysis of the benefits received by different groups is as follows:

Percentage Distribution of Original and Final Income (After Payment of Taxes and Receipt of Benefits) in 1980

Quantile Group	Original Income	Final Income
Top 20%	45	39
21%-40%	27	24
41%-60%	19	18
61%-80%	9	12
81%-100%	0.5	6.8
Total Income	100	100

Source: CSO *Economic Trends* no 339 January 1982 Table 11 p 100. Quoted in V George and P Wilding 1984 op cit p 111.

114. J Le Grand 1982 op cit p 150.
115. Ibid p 151.
116. T Raison (ed) *The Founding Fathers of Social Science* Penguin, Harmondswith 1969 p 40.
117. B Fay *Social Theory and Political Practice,* George Allen and Unwin, London 1980.
118. Ibid pp 42-3.
119. Ibid p 60.
120. Ibid p 80.
121. Ibid p 97.
122. Ibid p 97.
123. Ibid p 108.
124. The foreword to the published version of the report by the 1980 Secretary of State for Social Services dismisses the policy implications of the report as too expensive and probably ineffective. See P Townsend and N Davidson 1982 op cit.

Acknowledgements

The authors and publishers would like to thank the following for the use of copyright material:

A H Halsey, A F Heath and J M Judge for a table from *Origins and Destinations* (1980), Oxford University Press (Page 136); R Mishra for extracts taken from *Society and Social Policy: Theoretical Perspective on Welfare*, Macmillan, London and Basingstoke (Pages 114 and 121); D Harker for extracts taken from *One for the Money: Politics and the Popular Song*, Hutchinson Publishing Group Ltd (Pges 10-12); R Titmuss for material taken from *Gift Relationship* and J Le Grand for extracts taken from *Strategy of Equality*, George Allen & Unwin (Pages 151-154); HMSO for figures taken from table 8, page 33 of *National Dwelling and Housing Survey* (1979), and for figures taken from the *Annual Abstract of Statistics, Social Trends,* (1984), and *New Society* (1981), and for tables taken from Cmnd 8273 (1981) (Pages 44, 136, 139, 140). Extracts taken from page 221 of *Social Services of England and Wales* by Mary Penelope Hall, edited by J B May et al (1983), and extracts taken from *Suicide: A Study in Society* by E Durkheim (1979), and extracts taken from *Talcott, Parsons and the Social Image of Man* by K Menzies (1977) Routledge & Kegan Paul PLC (Pages 91, 45-48, 57, 72 18-20).

Despite every effort, the publishers have as yet been unable to obtain permission for the following:

Extracts taken from *Sociology and Social Policy* by P Townsend (1975) and extracts taken from *Housing Policy* by D Donnison and C Ungerson (1982), Penguin Books Ltd (Pages 98, 107, 109); Extracts taken from H Westergaard's *The Myth of Classlessness* in R Blackburn's *Ideology in Social Science* (1972) Fontana Books (Pages 115, 122-123); a table taken from *Inequality — Is it inevitable?* by J Brotherston in *Equalities and Inequalities in Health*, Table 8.17 (1976) by C O Carver and J Peel, Academic Press Inc Ltd (Page 134).

They ask the relevant copyright holders or their agents to contact them about this should the book succeed in coming into their hands.

167

SUBJECT INDEX

AUTHOR INDEX